TIKVAH

CHILDREN'S BOOK CREATORS
REFLECT ON HUMAN RIGHTS

SeaStar Books

New York

SEASTAR BOOKS
A division of NORTH-SOUTH BOOKS INC.

Published in the United States by SeaStar Books, a division of North-South Books Inc., New York.
Published simultaneously in Canada, Australia, and New Zealand by North-South Books,
an imprint of Nord-Süd Verlag AG, Gossau Zürich, Switzerland.
First published in 1999 by the University of Connecticut.

Library of Congress Cataloging-in-Publication Data is available.

ISBN 1-58717-097-3 (reinforced trade binding)
1 3 5 7 9 RT 10 8 6 4 2
ISBN 1-58717-098-1 (paperback binding)
1 3 5 7 9 PB 10 8 6 4 2

Printed in the U.S.A.

For more information about our books, and the authors and artists who create them, visit our web site:
www.northsouth.com

CONTENTS

Foreword

Tikvah, the Hebrew word for hope, expresses the clear interest that children's book illustrators have in human rights. The preservation and expansion of those rights is essential to a healthy world community as well as to the fullest appreciation of their artistic works. Children must dwell in a safe, nurturing environment in order to enjoy fully the wonderful images that illustrators create for them. A child's exposure to, and appreciation of, good books of all kinds at an early age helps that child develop an understanding of the importance of respecting the rights of others and of the basic social connections that we all share.

Tikvah provides forty-three of America's most distinguished contemporary children's book illustrators the opportunity to express their commitment to human rights in a publication intended primarily for an adult audience. The approaches, styles, and themes that the contributors have selected to state their views vary widely, and offer a balance between powerful and peaceful presentations. Each work embodies its own message; together they make a forceful statement about the critical importance of human rights. Taken as a whole they also clearly indicate the importance of freedom of expression as a critical element of human rights.

Tikvah was originally conceived as a special project in conjunction with the dedication of the Thomas J. Dodd Research Center at the University of Connecticut in Storrs, Connecticut. The Dodd Center houses the Northeast Children's Literature Collection (NCLC), which consists of a substantial body of late nineteenth- and twentieth-century illustrated American children's books. The collection also includes a large body of original materials from more than fifty contemporary children's authors and illustrators, a number of whom contributed to *Tikvah*.

Originally published as a limited edition, we are pleased to now be able to share these artists' powerful reflections with a general audience. Part of the royalties from the sale of this book will further the preservation and study of children's literature that the NCLC will continue to support in the twenty-first century. As recognition of the all-inclusive spirit of human-rights advocacy, the remaining portion of royalties will be donated to human-rights organizations of an international scope.

Books have the power to change lives. Doing so requires the remarkable creativity and insight of talented artists and writers as well as a willing audience. We are grateful to all of the contributors who took time from their busy schedules to provide the illustrations and words that constitute this book. We are also grateful to those who read, and share, this book with genuine concern and compassion.

Norman D. Stevens
Director of University Libraries, Emeritus
University of Connecticut

Introduction

Tikvah means hope and hope is represented by children. It is they who must justify our hope in education, human relations, and social justice. In other words: they represent our hope in a future which is an improvement on our past.

Children eternally evoke innocence and beauty. They are defenseless and harmless. They are frail and vulnerable. Is this why, in wars, they are the first victims? Adults hate one another and it is children who pay the price. Adults fight and children die. The first to be targeted for annihilation by the Nazis were the Jewish children, a million and a half of them. Was it that evil could not coexist with their purity?

Nothing is so despairing to some of us as the suffering of children, nor is anything as uplifting as the endeavor to help them in their conquest of happiness.

In this remarkable project, so aptly named *Tikvah,* adults will learn much from the visions of hope set forth by the prominent children's book illustrators, including two survivors of the Holocaust, who have contributed to it. The idea of having them illustrate their personal statements on important human rights issues works well. Making use of our memories of yesterday and today, they tell us how they visualize the world of tomorrow. Theirs and their children's.

In so doing, they become our teachers.

Elie Wiesel

TIKVAH

Social Justice
Natalie Babbitt

THIS LITTLE PICTURE does not describe the way things are but rather, the way I have always thought they ought to be. When I was a child I had, as we all do when we are very young, a strong sense of justice — a sense that was frequently violated by events large and small. I had no control over these events. That left me with a good deal of baffled outrage that has stayed with me and been continually reinforced throughout my life.

It is not so much legal justice that has concerned me. We do have a certain amount of control over that side of the situation, however feebly we seem to exercise it. Social justice is quite another matter. Nature herself — casual, disinterested Nature — seems to be the villain here. Some people are blessed with a bounty of beauty and intelligence and ability, while others struggle. Some people lead lives largely free of tragedy, while others are repeatedly scarred by it. Some people seem to come into this world equipped with peaceful, optimistic natures, while others seem born to fear and anxiety. Some people can do terrible things and get away with them every time, while others are caught and punished for the smallest infractions.

Curiously, no one seems to be fortunate, or unfortunate, in every category. Surely no family was ever endowed with more intelligence and ability than the Kennedy family, and yet tragedy has been a constant in their lives. I suppose it would be possible to say that this is an example of Nature keeping things even. Nature does not keep things even. Nature is demonstrably random, and blind to inequality. We must make a supreme effort to be tolerant, understanding, and patient with what cannot be changed, and try, through our social structures, to level things up as best we can.

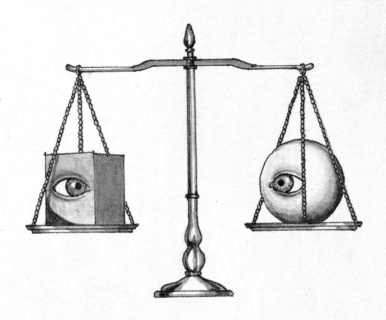

Brutalized Humanity
Leonard Baskin

Our human frame, our gutted mansion, our enveloping sack of beef and ash is yet a glory. Glorious in defining our universal sodality and glorious in defining our utter uniqueness. The human figure is the image of all. It contains all and it can express all. We have always created the human figure in our own image, and in our time that image is despoiled and debauched. I depict bruised and brutalized humanity, alone, naked, middle-aged, and defenseless. Our survival is the paradigm and our experience our fulfillment as life-filled creatures forcing earth to bloom and to yield peace. My work, a large part of it, has thematically dealt with the duality of tyrant and the tyrannized, expropriator and the expropriated, the powerful and the flayed victims of oppression, the arm of power. The forging of works of art is perhaps our last remaining semblance of divinity. We have been incapable of love, wanting in charity, and despairing of hope. We have not molded a life of abundance and peace and we have charred the earth and befouled the heavens more wantonly than ever before. We have made of Arden a landscape of death. In this garden I dwell, and in limning the horror, the degradation and the filth, I hold the cracked mirror up to humans. All previous art makes this course inevitable.

proof   Baskin

THE WOLF AND THE LAMB

Eric Carle

"*The wolf also shall dwell with the lamb, and the leopard shall lie down with the kid.*"

ISAIAH 11:6

Chicken's Choice
Normand L. Chartier

A SOMEHOW LESS than human class of beings; not fully humans; inferior humans; not worthy of lawful protection; therefore they can be owned, used, killed, experimented with, and body parts used to benefit the superior human beings. An existence reliant on being wanted, or not wanted, by the superior beings.

Herein are familiar excuses for the inhuman injustices of slavery, the horrors of the Holocaust, and other human rights miscarriages around the world. These same excuses are being utilized to the fullest today in the United States and in other countries. Under the banner of freedom of choice, or women's rights, over thirty million unborn human beings have been killed and discarded, or had their body parts "harvested," since the legalization of abortion in 1973. No matter the slogan, or the reason, removal of a fetus (Latin: young one) requires killing it.

Ironically, at least half of the eliminated unborn are female. It is women who are being exploited by the abortion industry. It is not socially, or politically, correct these days to point out this human injustice, by being a "voice for the voiceless." So be it. Here I quote two other voices.

Nobel Peace Prize winner Mother Teresa said, "Many people are very, very concerned with the children of India, with the children of Africa, where quite a few die of hunger, and so on. Many people are also concerned about the violence in this great country of the United States. These concerns are very good. But often these same people are not concerned with the millions who are being killed by the deliberate decisions of their own mothers. And this is what is the greatest destroyer of peace today — abortion, which brings people to such blindness."

As Theodore Geisel (Dr. Seuss) wrote in *Horton Hears a Who* — "A who is a who no matter how small."

Enjoying the River
Victoria Chess

On a fine Sunday afternoon in May, Isaac, Clea, Quinn, and Daniel had a glorious time in the river. The dog watched them. The grownups sat on the bank laughing, chatting, swatting bugs, and listening to the children, the birds, and the lovely sound of running water. This would not be possible in the month of July.

Many decades ago, the town of Washington sold the water rights of the Shepaug River to the city of Waterbury. There is plenty of water for all, yet things are being managed so carelessly that by full summer the river is nearly dry. This is only a small thing in a small place, but how sad it is that enjoyment of one of Connecticut's most beautiful rivers must only be an occasional privilege rather than a right.

CHANCE
Etienne Delessert

EVERYTHING IS A question of chance: the victims will become the tormentors. There is no logic, no reason, no learning, no redemption.

You must do unto others what you expect them to do unto you. This lies at the heart of human rights.

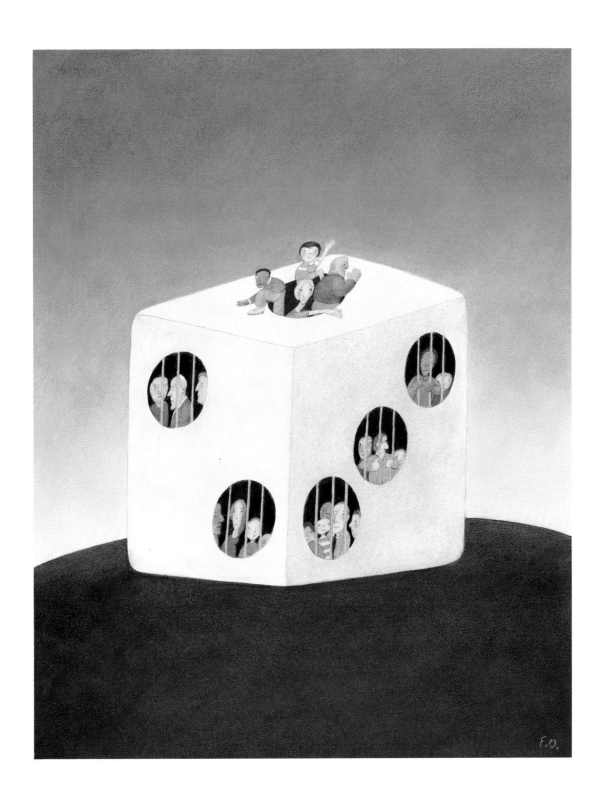

THE ART LESSON
Tomie dePaola

A CHILD'S FIRST confrontation with human rights can often occur at a very early age. Maybe not human rights in the larger context that involves racism, sexism, homophobia, ageism, "my-god-is-the-right-god-yours-isn't," or even "manifest destiny." Still I have a strong conviction that the attitude toward human rights that an individual carries within himself or herself is formed when very young.

All of us — Native Americans, Europeans, African Americans, Asians, Hispanics, Latinos, people of color (pink, blue, black, red, yellow, purple, orange, turquoise, lavender, magenta and everything else) — grow up seeing the universe through very subjective eyes — our own. We are told "No." We are told "Yes." We are fondled (hopefully), smacked (hopefully not), adored, and ignored. Babies, even babies of primates, experience all those things. Then comes the time for our education. And quite often that is the time for conformity.

Here I shift gears from us, we, and them and come down to me.

My older brother, for whatever reason, decided in my early childhood that my education under his tutelage would be, "I can do this and you can't." Ah, but I could do things he couldn't do, and I could do them easily. I could read. I could draw. I wasn't as pretty, but I could tap dance. So instead of helping me into the Mystery of School in 1940, he threatened me with it. Actually he did have the upper hand being older, stronger, and more experienced. (He was also a hawk during Vietnam. Surprise... I was a dove.) He let me know, with a chuckle, that school would whip the individuality out of me. He was almost right. They tried, oh my god they tried.

The image here has its roots in 1942. "All right class, we will all make a Christmas tree using our school crayons. The best ones will be hung in the hallway." Little Tommy's wasn't hung up because he drew an angel instead of a Christmas tree. The punishment meted out to individuals who are alone in their race, religion, sexual orientation, age, gender, and especially, their visions are indeed unfair. If you are not a team player and if you don't do, think and see the way the "team" does, then you have to sit on the sidelines. The team says so.

In my real and true life, the art teacher who came around every six weeks recognized me and my angel. I learned human rights from her. I was special because she was special. Just because neither of us fit into the mold didn't mean we weren't human and didn't have rights. I learned that in the 1940s. I've realized it in the 1990s.

PEACE
Jane Dyer

UNIVERSAL PEACE, more than anything else, is the long-term key to the elimination of the troubled environment in which too many of the world's children still struggle to survive. Peace truly lies at the heart of human rights.

Building a Better World
Cathryn Falwell

I wanted to make an image of children building a better world, using what they thought was important. I decided to ask kids what they thought children needed most. Here are their responses.

"Children need fun, education, and most of all, love."
Nicholas, age 9, USA

"A home."
Richard, age 8, Taiwan

"Toys, food, and clothes."
Kayana, age 5, Jamaica

"A mother giving them food."
Julio, age 6, Puerto Rico

"Attention, love, and friends."
Alexander, age 12, USA

"A family."
Inelise, age 8, USA

"School, water, Mom and Dad."
Wellington, age 9, Brazil

"Friends and school."
Ibrahim, age 8, Somalia

"Children need people being nice to them."
PiZhang, age 6, China

"Playing, exercise, to be taken care of, good food, and to be healthy. Oh! And L-O-V-E!"
Emerson, age 7, Brazil

ON BEING A BLACK MAN IN AMERICA
Tom Feelings

"Being a Black man in America is like having another job."
— Arthur Ashe

BEFORE THE HISTORIC 1963 March on Washington, DC, I literally missed the bus leaving my Brooklyn, New York neighborhood by fifteen minutes. To say the least, I was disappointed. Some thirty years later, in 1995, I sat listening to and watching on television various traditional civil rights activists, news commentators, clergymen, politicians, and Black conservatives express their doubts about the proposed Million Man March on Washington because this march was initiated by two controversial Black men whose views they opposed. Some said they could not support this march because of the involvement of these two "outsiders." Malcolm X's words flashed across my mind: "We are not fighting for integration or separation. We are fighting for recognition as free humans in this society." I began to wonder if it were these folks who were now missing this bus by misreading at a crucial point in history what the idea of a Million Man March might mean to the besieged spirits of Black men in America.

In the pit of my stomach I felt that this particular call for Black male unity was coming at a time when I, and we, need more than ever to see each other's faces up close and many times over. In our own way. On our own terms. Through our own eyes. Not as part of a gender mix or any kind of integrated group. Just us. Financed by us, supported by us, propelled by our own energy. Saying clearly to our loved ones, to each other, and to the world, that no, we were not like those demonized negative images that American society has projected onto us for centuries. Saying that we, as a large group of human beings, have done more than just survive oppression in all that time. In many ways, in many fields, level and unlevel, we have managed to flourish in spite of oppression. In the words of Paule Marshall, "We are a people who transformed humiliating experiences into creative ones."

Every day, as the Million Man March, drew closer, I experienced the growing conviction that this event was much more than just a good idea. It was a great idea whose time had come. So on October 15, 1995, with two brother-friends, I headed out for Washington, DC. On that profound, historic, cool morning of the 16th of October, we stood on steps looking out, and into, a vast flowing ocean of well over a million Black men. We felt an overwhelming affirmative connection with brothers young and old. We were seeing in those faces, near and far, the mirrored reflection of our collective power. We all basked in the warm, soulful glow of our ancestors' approval.

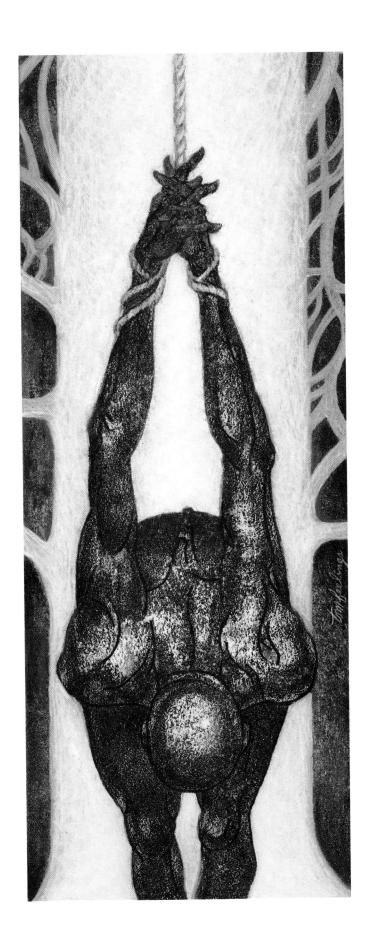

A CANDLESTICK OF PURE GOLD
Leonard Everett Fisher

"And thou shalt make a candlestick of pure gold... And there shall be six branches going out of the sides thereof; three branches of the candlestick out of one side thereof, and three branches of the candlestick out of the other side thereof... the whole of it one beaten work of pure gold."

EXODUS XXV: 31-36

THESE ARE THE instructions that G-d gave to Moses on Mt. Sinai for the creation of the seven lamp Menorah, Judaism's time-worn symbol of the eternal indestructibility of Jewish presence. From its conception in the Biblical past to the present, the seven lamp Menorah has symbolized not only that presence but also, when lighted and glowing, the seven days of Creation — with its promise of continuity of life.

Since the destruction of the Second Temple in Jerusalem by Titus and the Romans in 70 CE, the Menorah has come to signify life with freedom as divinely ordered. Its image can be seen on the Arch of Titus in Rome as the significant spoil of the Second Temple. Having stolen that symbol, the pagan Romans completed their humbling of the monotheistic Jewish people. But Titus came and went. The Romans of that classical time disappeared. The Jewish people survived them not only in body, but as an intractable spirit as well, — as they had the royal dynasties of Egypt earlier. They have outlived their tormentors over the centuries ever since. Even the indescribable immensity and horrendous toll of the modern Holocaust, a commitment to the absolute destruction of the Jewish people by Germany's Third Reich, could not overwhelm the Jewish will and life force. The Third Reich that was programmed for a thousand years into the future lasted but twelve. The architects of the Holocaust perished with it. The Jewish people survived them with their never-ending sufferings and their everlasting G-d given symbol of The Creation and life, the Menorah.

However synonymous with Judaism is the divinely inspired and historically ancient Menorah, the significance of this seven-lamp candelabra transcends its special Hebraic origins, connections, and nature. The Menorah has taken on a broader human rights symbolism — "life, liberty and the pursuit of happiness" — for all people regardless of race, religion, or politics. In a world so full with ignorance, darkness, and incomprehensible hate, the Menorah has become a symbol of light, hope and a more compassionate Almighty.

1995 – THE WAR AGAINST CHILDREN
Antonio Frasconi

DESPITE THE APPARENT progress that has been made in recent years on so many important human rights issues, there continues to be an unfortunate war against children that shows little sign of abating. Children are the innocent victims of the civil wars and famines, often interconnected, that still ravage the world. They toil long hours in substandard conditions to help support themselves and their families, producing goods from which others profit. Too many children have too little to look forward to.

The Help
Marylin Hafner

WE WERE AN ordinary, middle-class family weathering the depression years as so many millions of others did. That we had "Household Help" had something to do with the fact that my mother worked. It had more to do, I think, with my mother's sense of who she was. Brought up in a well-to-do bourgeois household, she never aspired to being a housewife. She chose to be a career woman and, although she worked hard, loved being out in the world. The times provided her with a never-ending supply of Southern Negro women who would work long hours for very little money. These colored women who moved through our lives provided me with security during my lonely pre-adolescence.

My parents were good people who surely must have been touched by the terrible disparity between the genteel poor and the truly needy, but somehow we children were never made aware of this gulf. It wasn't until twenty years later that I began to remember these kind, strong women and to separate them from the laundry basket and scrubbing brushes. I joined the marches against segregation without ever connecting the civil rights movement with the exploitation that existed in the Brooklyn of my childhood. I am glad that at long last I have the opportunity to say thank you to our "help."

They were various shades of delicious Brown: velvet-chocolate, beige & plum.
Beulah Violet Thelma Pearl just there to comfort
A solitary child.
The house was quiet when I came home from school, everyone still at their jobs.
My grandfather had moved out — too much noise he said.
She turned the cupboards out on Cleaning Day
My Mother's silver gleamed.
Hung sheets out on the lines & brought 'em in again.
The cellar stairs were scary.
Pearl baked seven-layer cakes, lemon pies,
And wasn't she the one known for her chicken fricassee?
My Father was a fussy eater — with a temper.
Mother was easy: she gave them clothes & extra food to take & never noticed corners.
Loved?
Beulah let me taste her coffee laced with sugar
And a half pint of heavy cream. She showed me
How to iron — and I know there were stories.
After all, there was all the afternoon with pot roast almost done.
I don't remember one.
Dinner cooked & served & dishes
Washed & dried by hand, they left on foot.
Thelma, did you live alone? How many children
Waited for their food until my Mother's forks were safely put away?
How many trolley cars & long blocks walked with swollen feet? We never knew.
Your life was lived in my spotless house
Entire. And when I wore a freshly-ironed dress
I never asked.

THE HELP c. 1935

MARYLIN HAFNER 1996

THE TERROR OF WARS
Michael Hague

THE RIGHT TO live free from the terror of wars is one of the most fundamental of all human rights. Wars are tragic human conflicts in which all basic human rights are sacrificed. As centuries of experience should have taught us, wars know no boundaries or limits. It is ultimately innocent individuals on both sides of all armed conflicts who must endure the death, destruction, grief, hunger, pain, suffering, and, above all, the loss of human dignity that wars inevitably create.

Child Labor

Lillian Hoban

When we think about child abuse, we most frequently are brought to tears by those horrifying cases that reach the newspapers. Cases where children are beaten to death, mutilated, tortured, or burned. There are other forms of child abuse that make the headlines only when celebrities are involved but are otherwise relegated to the occasional article written for the Sunday magazine section of a newspaper. Although not as dramatic as front-page stories, these forms of child abuse will probably have far longer and lasting effects on society.

In the United States child labor laws, on the surface, appear to have eradicated the use of under-age children in the work force. We smugly assume that it is only in countries that are not as enlightened as ours that children work long hard hours at back-breaking jobs and are understandably horrified to learn of such abuse in Third World countries. We are loath to admit it continues to exist in the United States. On the east and west coasts, and wherever there are large industrialized cities ringed round by suburbs, very young children work up to sixteen hours a day under intolerable conditions. Work is farmed out by factories to intermediaries who set up sweat shops that employ women and children at sub-standard wages. These facilities are frequently ill-lit, poorly ventilated, and have inadequate toilets, or none at all. Women workers are usually illiterate. Since the children labor from dawn until far into the night, they have little or no chance of an education. They are abused not only physically but emotionally and spiritually as well.

As we work to eliminate child labor in other countries, we must examine the issue in our own country.

A Glorious Array

Nonny Hogrogian

I OFTEN WONDER why some of us want everyone to be just like we are. We want people to have the same level of intelligence we have. We want people to have interests similar to our own. We want people to be the same color. We want everyone to conform to our idea of what is good.

Why, I wonder.

Is it fear that makes us think this way? Do we want only one color in our neighborhoods because it makes us feel safe?

We are who we are. Each person is an individual. Each of us chooses our own particular path. We come in many colors. We bring to one another new foods to eat, new thoughts to ponder, and new music for our ears. All of this makes our life here on earth infinitely more interesting.

Together we are a glorious array of colors, creativity, and taste. When we really know that, we will be able to celebrate our Oneness. We are one family that God has created.

PATRIARCHY AND TECHNOLOGY
Trina Schart Hyman

WHAT IS HAPPENING HERE?

Maybe she who is being taken apart and poisoned is an angel or mythological creature, or perhaps she is just a woman who happened to grow wings. The men are doctors, but they could just as easily be priests, or soldiers, or politicians.

These men have decided to cut away and destroy all the things about this creature that frighten or threaten them. Her breasts, because they nurture. Her wings, which are spirit and imagination. Her womb, because it brings forth new life. They have poisoned her with their chemicals, so her hair is gone and her mind and eyes are dead. They believe that as soon as they cut off her remaining wing, she may have a better chance for "life," with their help — if she survives.

The names of the two doctors are Patriarchy and Technology. The name of the patient is yours to choose. Maybe it's Earth or Mother Nature, or Emerging Country, or Suffer-the-Children. The doctors are convinced that they are right; that they know best. They seem concerned about the patient but this is only because their professional reputations must not be questioned. It's a matter of pride, and money, and power. If the patient dies or cannot "adjust," this isn't their fault. Besides, there are many more out there waiting. Many more who need their help and intervention, and they can make a bundle of money, too. Invasive procedures are required, unfortunately. Let's put the big machines to work; our computers know best. Let's get our heavy equipment in here to do the job faster. Time is money! Call in the big guns, get the artillery moving, put it on the Internet! Bulldoze those trees because they're in our way; get that woman. She's the enemy. Kill that baby — he's the enemy too. Because they gotta know who's *boss*, here! Call in the media, put it on TV, get it down on film, let's do a CD-ROM, and lie if you have to!

The doctors, the priests, the soldiers, the politicians, the industrialists; men with power and money. They're the *boss* here.

I could have made the angel in my picture black or brown, but I don't think that it matters much. The men who are destroying her share the same skin color. We all share the same skin, and the beautiful variations of its colors matter only when patriarchy and technology decide what is best for us. Their money and power is at stake, and their fear of the "other". All people, when they're cut, bleed the same color. We all bleed; we can all be tortured and killed if we are designated for the role of "other," and we are captured. The ones with nurturing bodies and minds go first. The gentle ones, the trusting ones; the ones with wings to fly. And we are most often mutilated, tortured, and killed by the ones we were schooled to trust. "Trust me! This is for your own good! Your welfare is our concern. Don't question, don't ask, don't think. Trust in us and in God the Father. Shut up! Stop fighting it! Lie down and stop screaming! We know what is best for you."

Mom? Mommy!

"Human rights" is a concept that simply doesn't exist. History, especially recent history, tells me otherwise. "Man rights" — money and power, patriarchy and technology rights; these are the things that shape our world and are now destroying it. I think that some of us understand this. It's been beaten into us in many ways, for thousands of years. It's a part of our education, and we have to adapt and adjust. We are used to being hunted down, questioned, imprisoned, tortured, and killed. Those of us with wings will hide them when we must, and show them when we can. We sometimes recognize one another and try to transmit courage. It's all we can do; perhaps we'll survive.

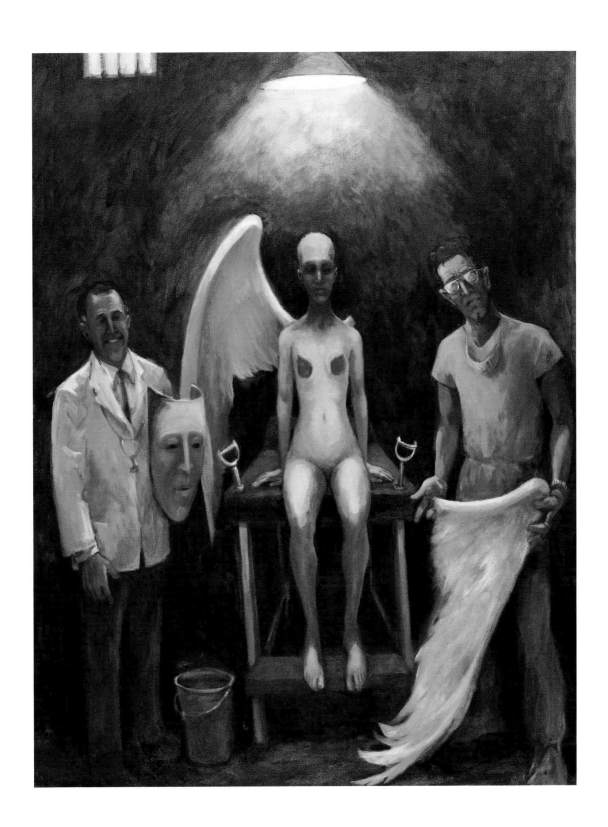

Haven Small
William Joyce

Integration of the public schools in Louisiana began in earnest the year I started middle school. I was thirteen years old and these would be the first Black kids I had ever met.

All the grownups were very tense. Parents. Newscasters. Newspaper reporters. Police. Teachers. Ministers. Everybody over five feet tall and of voting age looked ready for Armageddon.

The big day came. The grownup world held its breath... and nothing happened. Or at least nothing they expected. A bunch of kids just went to school. They got along. They learned together. They played together. Everything was cool.

Haven Small, a fellow thirteen year old, fell into our group as naturally and as easily as a breeze. His color had no more place in our thoughts than if he'd had freckles. He came home with me one day. My parents were very nice but after Haven left they told me in no uncertain terms that a Black kid was not welcome in our house. Not now. Not ever. I felt something inside I still cannot put into words. I told them I was embarrassed by them. I'd thought they weren't like that. I'd thought they were better than that. There was a long afternoon of quiet in our house. At dinner they apologized. They told me that from now on Haven, or any other friend of mine, was welcome in our home. Times had changed and they would change with them, they said.

Whatever failings my parents carried, they had taught me to stand up for what I thought was right and they had listened on the rare times I had grievances. Their calm capitulation, however, surprised even me. I guess it really was time for things to change.

After school, a few days later, our group drifted to the house of another classmate. Her father greeted us at the door and ordered us to leave. His daughter was not allowed to have boys over. His tone was stern, unkind, almost hateful. We wandered away. We knew the real reason why he made us leave. Even worse, Haven knew why too. I'll never forget the look on Haven's face. Wounded and humiliated, he had a sadness I could witness but never fully understand. Things like that didn't happen to white kids.

At my home a small victory had been won. Down the street a bitter enemy of equality and kindness had held his ground. I don't know if bigotry will ever completely disappear, but every small victory chips away at this blight on our better natures. Someday, with luck and perseverance, no thirteen year old will ever be made to feel that low again.

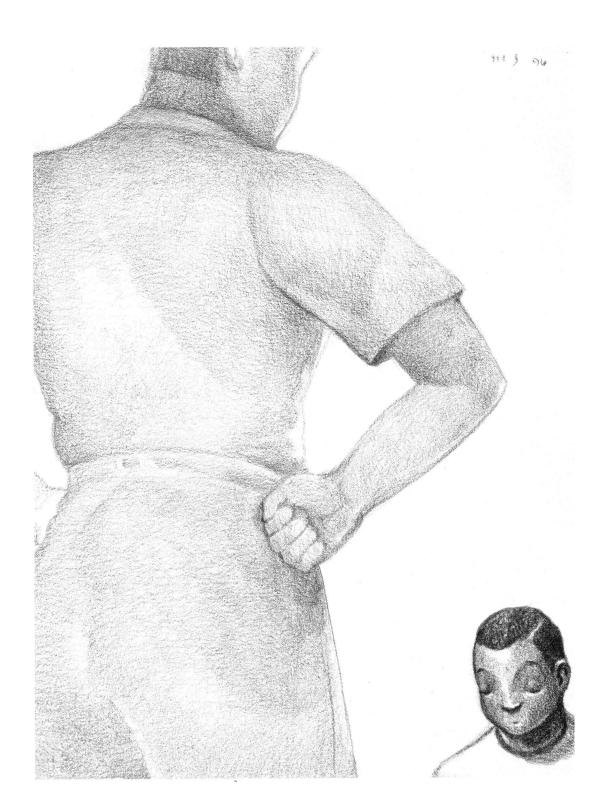

Merging with Nature
Steven Kellogg

When I was growing up in Norton Heights, Connecticut during the 1950s, one of the of the town's last surviving woodlands was located a block from the end of my driveway. How I treasured that piece of real estate! I can vividly recall the exhilaration I felt when I left the asphalt and the roadside weeds behind, to disappear into those densely treed acres. That transformation resonated within me like an escape from urban sterility to the mysterious and intriguing depths of the forest primeval. When neighborhood friends and I slipped along the sun dappled and darkly shadowed paths, our imaginations transformed us into tribesmen in the Amazon jungle, or explorers probing the frontiers of an undiscovered continent, or the resident wolf pack in a Nordic wilderness. Whenever I entered that fragment of undisturbed nature, the mysterious, magical, and liberating influence that it had upon my spirit was both exhilarating and tranquilizing. In my early forays into the world of art, I tried to imbue my pictures with the sense of wonder I felt in the presence of the shifting light patterns, the dark and mesmerizing variety of growing, living things, and the intriguing mysteries of those woods. The hints of deeper currents in the profound silence of the woodland caused me to lose myself in speculation and fantasy. They gave me a sense of a deeply satisfying oneness with nature, and feeling for an energy beyond the universe that was responsible for all that I saw and experienced. I knew that this touchstone would always be an important source of reassurance and healing. I have tried to structure my life so that withdrawal into the compelling serenity and grandeur of nature has always been available to me.

That emotional merging with nature, which moved me so deeply in my boyhood, moves me still. It is my hope that we, as a society, will recognize that access to the restorative influence and spiritual enlightenment that interaction with nature offers is a right that must be made available to those who pass this way after we have moved on. We must emulate the far sighted leaders at the end of the last century who decreed that the vast, pristine forest lands that encompass the Adirondack Mountains shall remain forever wild. They wanted nature to flourish there without disturbance so that successive generations could continue forever to wonder at and be nurtured by its magnificence.

Holidays
Hilary Knight

Two small children live next door to each other. A little girl lights her Hanukkah candle. A little boy reads a poem about a Christmas tree. Each in his or her own home shares the spirit of a unique and special holiday.

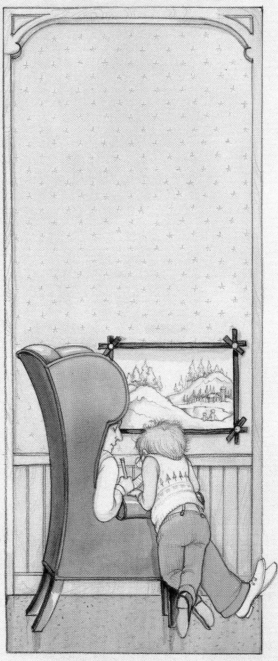

A Hunger for Knowledge
E. B. Lewis

When considering the subject of human rights I inevitably reach back into my formative years and emphasize the right of every child to accessible, quality education without discrimination based on race, religion or economic status.

My mother and father raised me, an African American boy growing up in Philadelphia, to believe that a good education was the most important achievement in life. They told me that with this accomplishment there was nothing I couldn't do. Along with this sound parental advice there were disturbing reports in the media about young Blacks being harassed and beaten for attempting to seek better educational opportunities in predominantly white schools. Those Blacks were literally in jeopardy of losing their lives. I drew the conclusion that the consequences of following my parents' advice could cost me my life.

Did I not have the right to pursue the best education possible? Was I not deserving of the same privileges as others? At a tender age the roots of inferiority can stem from discrimination. Ultimately one questions what one's rights are as a human being.

In spite of the obstacles of racism, I was blessed and got through my educational experiences. Even in adulthood I continue to encounter the victims of that same irrational system. My friends who have taken up the reins of educating our youth in inner city schools express their outrage at not being able to obtain something even as simple as construction paper for art classes. Adequate books and other materials essential to learning are hard to come by. By allowing this elite selectiveness to exist, based on economics, accessibility, race, or creed, we are cementing the fate of the less fortunate. They may never break down the walls of ignorance and travel through the worlds of knowledge that computers, books, and related materials provide.

Being a part of the industry that creates children's books, I've grown more passionate in my belief that quality education be free and available to all as part of the human right to pursue knowledge. In a trip to Ethiopia I was deeply moved by the eagerness of a young child, as his eyes poured over the pictures in one of my books. His hunger for knowledge was as intense as his hunger for food. Is he not deserving to pursue knowledge? Is he not also a human being?

THE PEOPLE OF LAPANÓW

Anita Lobel

IT WAS PASSOVER time again. Spring 1942. In Lapanów, Poland. Passover celebrations were no longer allowed. "Verboten" was the German word heard over and over. The Jewish people in the village were preparing in secret. Mazzohs had been baked.

"They will be going to all the Jewish houses," a Polish man came to warn us.

Çioçia Lelia came to me one morning. "You have to be a big girl," she said. "You can help us keep a secret." I had a doll carriage. It was large and deep. Niania was angry. She saw no reason why mazzohs were so important. "Jews," she muttered. Çioçia ignored Niania and piled the mazzohs into the doll carriage. We put my dolls on top and covered everything with a heavy blanket. The day was cold and wet. I was bundled up. Heavy felt boots. Coat. Hat over my ears. A scarf wrapped around my neck and over my mouth.

The earth of the fields behind the house was muddy. The wheels of the doll carriage kept sinking down deep. Getting stuck. I worried that the carriage would topple over and all the mazzohs would spill out in plain sight into the mud. I tried to be careful. But if I were too careful I would look suspicious. Behind me, at our house and at other houses, too I heard the Germans. They didn't sound dangerous. They just sounded like bullies who knew they were stronger than the people they were pushing around.

My woolen scarf itched. I did not stop walking and wheeling the carriage. I even began to sing to myself. As if I were a mother rocking her babies to sleep. Just like Niania, I did not care about the mazzohs. It was too late now. I did not want to get caught.

I heard two Germans behind coming closer.

"Was hast du da?" one said pointing to the carriage. I guessed what he meant. I answered in Polish, "To sa, moje lalki." He could have just poked his rifle barrel under the blanket. Instead he shrugged his shoulders and continued through the field to the next Jew House.

The two Germans were young and handsome. So much better looking than my long nosed, droopy eyed cousin. The one who slaughtered chickens. So much better looking than the short sweaty man who sometimes came to visit homely Çioçia Lelia. He never bothered taking off the round black cap from on top of his kinky hair. But I couldn't think of the Germans as real people. I couldn't separate them from their uniforms and their rifles. Why did they believe me? Why would I be wandering around alone, pushing a doll carriage through a muddy field?

After the soldiers left I kept walking back and forth until Niania came to get me. She hurried me and my doll carriage through a side door back to the house. Çioçia took the mazzoh bundle and hid it somewhere. I was happy to be rid of the mazzohs. I was happy to be back with Niania.

It was not long after this Passover that we began to hear rumors of roundups in nearby villages. Niania knew that it would not be long before the Jews of Lapanów would be on the lists. She decided that from then on it would be safer for my brother to dress as a girl. She had not been back to her own village for many years. That was where we moved on to. There were no Jews there. Niania's story would be that her husband had been killed. That she was returning home with her two daughters.

I never saw the people from Lapanów again.

THE YOUNG ARTIST
Thomas Locker

THE YOUNG ARTIST (Dial Books, 1989) is about the artist's struggle to maintain his right to self expression and self realization. He really wants to paint the light on the land. The people want him to paint pictures of themselves as they want to be, rather than as they are. This is a classic conflict between the artist and the realities of the market.

The book is personal and somewhat autobiographical. After many years of direct political involvement, I have withdrawn from such direct involvement with human rights issues to find meaning in thinking about and painting nature. A sense of reverence for the natural world is the starting place for all rights created by human institutions.

THE WORLD'S RELIGIONS
Betsy & Giulio Maestro

RELIGIOUS FREEDOM DEPENDS on tolerance. Luckily, tolerance can be taught. It is incumbent upon us all to ensure the future of religious freedom in our world by teaching tolerance. Children must be the pupils in a new and energized effort to establish tolerance and respect for one another as a new world order.

Tolerance and respect come from understanding and knowledge. All over the world, people are following countless paths to Enlightenment, Truth, Paradise, and Heaven. Although some believe that their way is the one right way, in fact, there is no one right way to seek God. There are hundreds of answers to the questions that humans have wondered about since the beginning of time. The answers and the right way for Buddhists are not the same as the answers and right way for Muslims.

Isn't it interesting to live in a world of such rich diversity? Despite all of our differences, the people of the world share many ideas and feelings. The strength and comfort that humans draw from the practice of their faiths is much the same the world over. How reassuring it is to discover that the Golden Rule, stated in many different ways, is part of most of the world's religions. These connections can help children to understand that we are all part of the same story and that each of our individual threads are part of the same cloth.

Intolerance equals tragedy. Intolerance has been at the root of persecution and violence throughout human history. Intolerance is born of fear and ignorance. It can be eradicated by knowledge. We need to educate our children. We need to help them learn about the beliefs of others. We need to show them how to appreciate the similarities that we share, and to accept the differences that divide us. Understanding and respecting the beliefs and customs of others does not in any way diminish our own convictions. When all people are truly neighbors, living each day by the Golden Rule, peace and love can flourish on earth. Shouldn't this be the true goal of every religion?

The Brickyard
Marianna Mayer

THE CHILDREN IN America who enjoy the lavishly illustrated children's books that we work so hard to produce are far removed from the nineteenth century Dickensian world of child labor. Yet the UN's International Labor Organization estimates that around the world as many as 200 million children under the age of 14 go to work rather than school. Youngsters in developing nations are making everything from clothing, shoes, handbags, and carpets to children's toys, soccer balls, and yes — even children's books; products that will find their way into America's stores and catalogues.

These unfortunate children are the dark side of the new global economy. They are an international underclass working 12 or more hours a day, six or seven days a week. In the brickyards of Nepal, they are forced to carry heavy loads. In the leather handbag plants of Thailand, over-worked children are forced to ingest amphetamines so that they will work quickly. In the charcoal industry of Brazil, tens of thousands of children work in a sooty infernos producing ingredients for the steel alloys used in the manufacture of American cars.

Child laborers everywhere develop arthritis and carpal tunnel syndrome from repetitive work; their respiratory systems are damaged by inhaling toxic chemicals in poorly ventilated workshops; their posture is permanently altered by long hours in cramped conditions. The chains that bind us to these children are nearly invisible. As consumers we search for that perfect mix of high quality and low prices — oblivious to the wasted childhood that makes such bargains possible. Behind many of the cleverly manufactured paper products, toys, clothing, found in abundance on the American market are children. Who are they? They are faceless; they are not represented by the "Made in Pakistan" (or India, Honduras, or Mexico) labels carried, like exotic travel stickers, on the many products that we buy unthinkingly.

To learn more, and to make a difference, contact electronic sources such as PeaceNet's section on Children's Rights (http://www.igc.org/issues/educat/#childrights). At Children's Rights Networking @ IGC, kids can speak to kids about themselves, their families, schools, activities, and can explore global issues such as child labor and the protection of the environment

No Internet access? Write: Child Labor Coalition, c/o National Consumers League, 1701 K Street N. W., Suite 1200, Washington, DC 20006, or call them at 202-835-3323.

Privacy and Possibility
Emily Arnold McCully

HUMAN RIGHTS ARE challenged in every generation and their defenders will always be in the minority. Since human rights don't confer quantifiable benefits on society, they depend on enlightenment, which itself depends on imagination.

We measure a society's success not in numbers but in liberties. Everyone wants a "better life," greater comforts. Few of us bother to imagine the way others live, and rise to their defense. If profit, efficiency, safety, and self reliance are to rule over imagination, how will human rights survive?

Children are easily encouraged to imagine what it would feel like to live someone else's more difficult life because they are so concerned with fairness. But even in childhood, imagination is threatened. More than adults, children are subjected to noise and junk. They are constantly supervised or painfully neglected. They are warned against the world or prematurely flung into it. Few have the freedom simply to wonder but such wondering develops individual defenders of human rights.

My elder child, who is pictured here, used to sit and watch leaves falling for hours, dreaming, wondering — securely adrift in nature, privacy, and possibility.

Free at Last?
Michael McCurdy

HUMAN RIGHTS IS an issue that inevitably involves all races and ethnic backgrounds. After all, injustice is forever—and everywhere—with us. On a personal level, I always connect this issue to American racism and, especially, to the plight, past and present, of the African American in our society.

I have always had an affinity for Black culture and an empathy for African Americans - their history, their heroes, their pivotal link with our Civil War. In the 1960s I was involved, in my own small way, in the civil rights movement. I lacked the money to take buses south for marches or for rallies in Washington, but I did participate in Martin Luther King's exciting walk through Boston in April 1965. There, people marched in the rain from Roxbury to hear Dr. King's ringing pleas for justice, under the trees of Boston Common. A little later, as a member of the Society of Friends, I was active in the civil rights crusade and in protesting against the absurdity of the Vietnam War.

The man in my drawing appears to be an African American, but he could be anyone who has broken free from the shackles of persecution and bondage. He has struggled to make his way out of the rock pile, and out of the pit, into brighter fields ahead. I hope he makes it.

THE LITTLE MATCH GIRL
Lauren Mills

MANY PEOPLE MAY feel that Andersen's story *The Little Match Girl* is too sad and frightening to read to children. It is, after all, about extreme poverty and child abuse. A little girl with no coat or shoes is made to sell matches in the snowy streets. She is so afraid of being beaten by her father for being unable to sell them that she chooses to stay in the streets, and freezes to death. Such harsh reality we can read about in today's news. Still this story has the essential elements of a fairy tale that transforms adversity into hope and love.

Bruno Bettleheim says that fairy tales offer reassurance to children and empower those who feel helpless. Imaginary characters with other-worldly qualities aid the child when no one else can. Fairy tales serve children in the same way that religious and mythical stories serve adults. They provide ways to find meaning and to sort out difficulties; they offer hope.

I am attracted to *The Little Match Girl* because the child's own imagination, or spiritual faith, releases her from her sadness and suffering. She has not chosen death over life, for she does not realize she is dying as she strikes match after match to see her beautiful visions. Her death, and adults' misunderstanding of it, is society's punishment for allowing the tragedy to happen.

In Andersen's words, "The little girl was found in the corner between the two houses in the cold light of dawn. Her cheeks were red and there was a smile on her lips, but she was dead, frozen to death on the last evening of the old year. The sun of New Year's Day rose over the little body as she sat there with the bundle of burnt matches. 'Trying to keep warm,' they said. No one knew what beautiful visions she had seen, or how she and her grandmother had gone away into the glory and joy of the New Year."

As long as there is horror, child abuse, meaningless poverty, and starvation, our souls and spirits must be nourished and guided by fairy tales, myths, and religious stories so that we can persevere.

After the Storm
Wendell Minor

Gandhi once stated that "truth resides in every human heart, and one has to search for it there and be guided by truth as one sees it. But no one has a right to coerce others to act according to his own view of truth."

The issue of human rights, for me, is one of truth: the ability of individuals to discover within themselves their true identity. By discovering one's true identity, one discovers self respect. Without self respect, respect for others is not possible. The search for a true identity is conducted not only from within, but also from without, in relationship to the natural world. Man's connection to nature and the basic elements of life is undeniable. Unfortunately, as we look toward the new century, that conduit to our origins has been lost to many.

Our hope of ever relating to one another in a gesture of mutual respect is directly related to our capacity to respect nature. If we lose our connection to nature we lose our humanity, along with any hope of achieving the noble goal of harmony among all humans and among all living things.

As an artist, it has been my mission to bring to children my 'truth,' by sharing my view of the natural world in picture books exploring our great country. When I was a child, my father shared his love of nature with me. It was a great gift, a gift that I want to share with many generations to come.

One of the most beautiful sights in nature is the rainbow that follows a thunderstorm. It is a sign that even in our darkest moments of despair, there is hope. Where there is hope there is the chance we can seek our own truth; the truth that is the rock of human dignity.

THE DEATH OF ABEL
Barry Moser

"And it came to pass, when they were in the field, that Cain rose up against Abel his brother, and slew him. ¶ And the Lord said unto Cain: 'Where is Abel thy brother?' And he said: 'I know not; Am I my brother's keeper?' "

GENESIS 4:8 – 9

HANSEL AND GRETEL
Dennis Nolan

THE GRIMM'S *Hansel and Gretel* contains a great richness of fantasy elements that make it an appealing tale to tell. The beautiful snow-white bird leads the children to the cottage made of cake and sugar; the frightening witch of the enchanted wood is overpowered by Gretel; the children return home with caskets of pearls and precious stones. All of this happens in a time and place far removed from our everyday life. That the cruel, heartless abandonment of Hansel and Gretel at the start of the story reads uncomfortably realistic and contemporary, is a sad commentary on the state of humanity and our still aching need to care for and nurture our children.

HANSEL & GRETEL

IN THE PENAL COLONY, 1920
Robert Andrew Parker

"'Be Just!' is what is written there,' said the officer once more. 'Maybe,' said the explorer, 'I am prepared to believe you.'"

— FRANZ KAFKA, from *The Penal Colony*

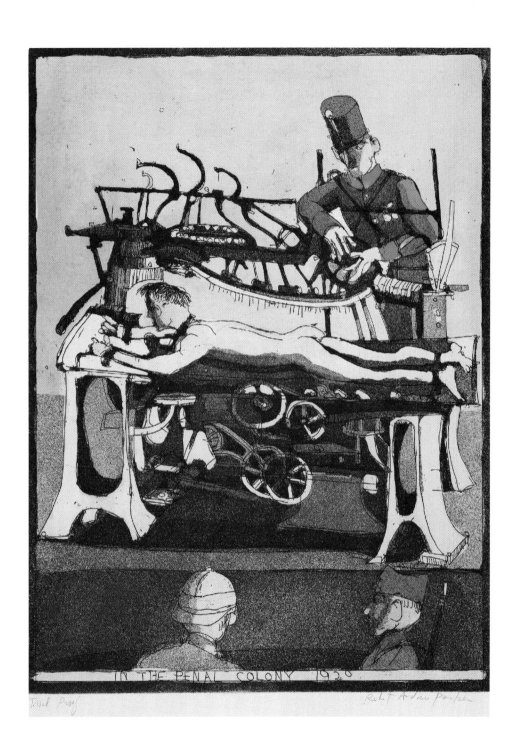

IN THE PENAL COLONY 1920

I Want to Dream a Rainbow

Gloria Jean & Jerry Pinkney

A FIRST THOUGHT on the subject of human rights came with a word: hunger. Children living without food. Too often have we witnessed this growing problem, in news magazines, on television, and through the numerous requests for help that we receive. Hunger is a deep concern to us. Again and again we are rocked by the plight of unfed children.

We participated in an outreach program affiliated with an exhibition that Jerry curated on children's books. We made presentations in classrooms and libraries. It was disturbing to find few up-to-date books on school shelves, and to see how uninspiring were the learning facilities. The word "hunger" again entered our thoughts. We asked ourselves, "Can children become positive, contributing adults if they are deprived of food for their stomachs or for their minds? How can their dreams flourish? Without learning tools and a healthy diet, what will happen to their ideas? How will these children be able to participate?"

In Jerry's painting, "I Want to Dream a Rainbow," our grandson Myles Leon Pinkney, the model, is positioned in the corner of a darkened room. He is holding onto a good book, which is lighted by a rainbow. He has found in his reading place a safe space to discover dreams, hopes, and aspirations.

As caring individuals we must attend to the physical, mental, and spiritual health of our children. We must continue to share with those who "have not" by feeding their bodies and minds. This portrayal of one child, holding onto one book speaks to us of a need to see that every child has the nourishment needed for a future filled with attainable possibilities.

"I want to dream a rainbow," the child says. Let's give all children the chance to make their dreams their realities.

DOCTOR-ASSISTED DEATH
Mark Podwal

THE ISSUE OF physicians taking an active role in ending the lives of their patients is fraught with moral dilemma. For some, doctor-assisted death, like abortion, is merely a matter of personal freedom. For others, the ending of lives without patients' consent recalls one of the most barbarous state-sanctioned crimes in modern history, the euthanasia program of Nazi Germany.

Sixty years ago, Nazi physicians, violating the ethical standards they had sworn to uphold, murdered the mentally ill and severely handicapped. They rationalized the killing of more than seventy thousand people as "acts of compassion." Initially, starvation was used to end "life unworthy of living." In time, lethal injection and gassing became the preferred methods of extermination. Families of the victims received falsified death certificates. One doctor whose career began in the euthanasia program became the commandant of Treblinka. At Auschwitz, life or death was often decreed by a flick of a doctor's finger.

Supporters of euthanasia will characterize the Nazi's wholesale slaughter of the mentally ill and handicapped as an abhorrent aberration. Yet no matter how the circumstances are defined for legitimate physician-assisted death, restraints cannot always protect the rights of those who might not want to die. Walter Reich, a psychiatrist and director of the United States Memorial Holocaust Museum, has written that killing as a legitimate medical procedure "may well erode the identities of physicians as healers, turn some into socially sanctioned killers and undermine the trust that all of us must have — especially when we're desperately ill and want to live— that our doctors are agents of life, not death."

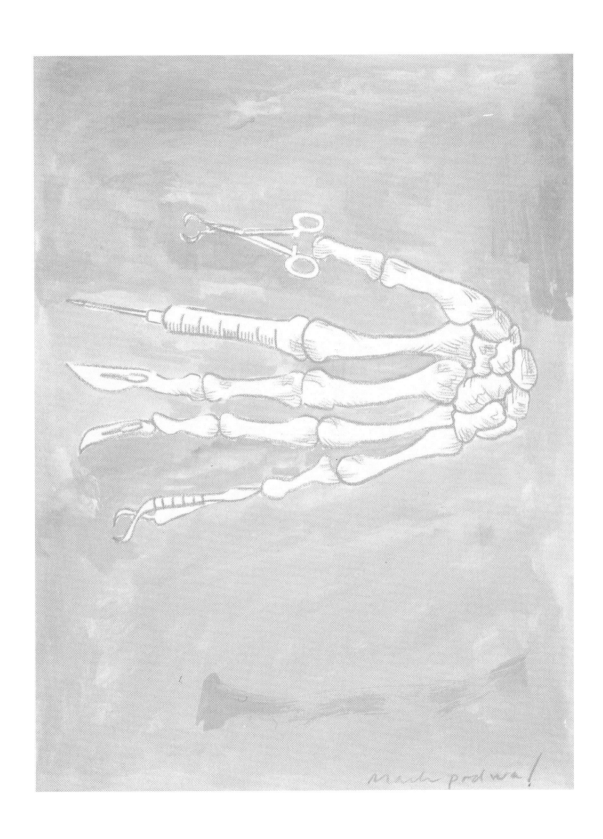

Mach podwa!

Human Dignity
Anita Riggio

In *Beloved,* Toni Morrison writes of Baby Suggs, "Who decided that, because slave life had 'busted her legs, back, head, eyes, hands, kidneys, womb and tongue,' she had nothing left to make a living with but her heart — which she put to work at once."

When we speak of human rights, we speak of human dignity and the capacity of the human heart to transcend injustice through hope, forgiveness, and love.

Portrait of a Child: Unborn

Ruth Sanderson

I WOULD LIKE to share my perspective on members of humanity who have no rights and no voice of their own — unborn children. I believe we are made, from the moment of conception, in the image and likeness of God. Abortion is the greatest evil occurring in the world today.

Listen for a moment to the expressions we use regarding pregnancy: the woman is "with child," she is "expecting." We proclaim the unborn child's humanity from the moment of conception! All that is required is time for the expectation to be fulfilled. The argument that the woman should have control over what she does with her body is, to my mind, absurd. We are talking about a sacred trust here. It is another life over which the pregnant woman has "control." How can we presume to say that we have the right to end lives that are just beginning? A "fetus" is not fully developed, and, therefore, not "human," some say. New born babies aren't fully developed either. They can't walk or talk. Still we know that in time they will develop into full-grown adults. We do not kill infants even though they are not mature, functioning human beings. Isn't the unborn child as deserving of life as the undeveloped infant?

Granted, for some it is easy to think about the child in the womb as a lump of tissue and not the essence of humanity. People have always been able to avoid seeing the obvious. We have a tendency to deaden our hearts against atrocities of all kinds. This project would not have been conceived if this were not so.

Sanderson '96

HOPE
Uri Shulevitz

THIS PICTURE IS a symbolic evocation of my childhood memories from World War II. It shows the ruins of a house at dawn. Humans built it and destroyed it. The choice is in their hands. Yet life goes on. Where there is life, there is hope for a better tomorrow. "Sad soul, take comfort, nor forget that sunrise never failed us yet." (Celia Laighton Thaxter *1835-94*).

THE CHINESE PRISONER
Marc Simont

IN A COMPETITIVE world, taking a stand against violators of human rights is not simple. An acceptable approach towards Cuba (who needs cigars?) would not work in Saudi Arabia (we need oil). If Castro gets upset there is rejoicing in Congress and Miami, but if the king of Saudi Arabia, who still believes in slavery, shows displeasure, the market shivers.

China is anxious to do business with the western world but gets very touchy on the subject of Tiananmen Square and its orphans. National pride runs high. If some other government were to point a finger at our homeless, or the murder rate in our cities, we'd be quick to say internal affairs are off limits.

The best thing we can do to further human rights, for starters, is pay our full dues to the United Nations and to support its initiatives. Contributing to an international consensus gives us more clout and reduces the glare of individual exposure.

Signing a Petition
Esphyr Slobodkina

THE FORMATIVE YEARS of childhood are brief but very important.

Parents, teachers, librarians, and — yes — writers and illustrators of children's books should take their responsibility very seriously; for the images, the verbal patterns, and the kinds of behavior they present to children are likely to influence them for the rest of their lives. Similarly, refined, or vulgar, choices in clothes, in furnishings, and in works of art are likely to reflect the discriminating, or careless attitude, of the child's early mentors.

Aesthetic impressions, like early moral teachings, are indelible. They, consciously or unconsciously, form the bedrock upon which (or in opposition to which) a person's spiritual existence will rest.

Good taste, like good speech and high moral principles, is a hard thing to define. In addition, it is highly controversial. I can, and do, urge parents to be as determined as possible in keeping to a minimum the amount of "amusing trash" in their children's intellectual diet. Do leave a little room for contact with things of serene beauty and ideas of true worth! Don't forget that exposure to beauty and ideas may stand them in good stead in the future as a peaceful oasis in times of extreme stress and anxiety.

Many a dull job or sleepless night can be lightened considerably by remembering the lovely, rhythmic prose of some folk tale or children's poem. Early contact with vivid, worthwhile art makes it as pleasant to remember in later years as to look at in childhood, and trains the eye to seek the harmonious instead of the absurd and bizarre. It enables us to pick out among the surrounding everyday scenes and combinations of objects those which soothe and satisfy rather than jar and irritate.

All these are very useful protection against the progressively complicated and disquieting world our children are condemned to meet.

Your Kind
Jos. A. Smith

THE GREATEST THREAT we pose to each other is a fruit of our sublime ability to generalize.

The capacity to manipulate symbols — the root of our talent to learn and theorize — is also the source of our art.

And ah, see how creatively we use it!

After all, let me transform you into an abstraction and I have permission to deprive you of your basic rights, your freedoms, even (and this is really only another small step) your life.

As long as I see you as a person, I'm lost. If you remain someone who has needs, who laughs and cries, and who feels pleasure or pain, I see a real person who might stop to pet a dog or marvel at a poem. It's too easy to care for you. I might even be tempted to share what I have with you.

Let me turn you into a symbol and you are nothing but a label. I push you back to an emotional distance beyond my power to focus. The details that made you real disappear. You blend into a faceless group I can call "Your Kind."

Thank God I'm not one of "Your Kind."

As long as we divide people into "Us" and "Them," let's not pretend to be surprised when evil smiles back at us from the mirror.

Joy!

Cyndy Szekeres

HUMAN RIGHTS, in a simple definition: the ability to enjoy life, the expectation that others will respect that right, the conviction to maintain such a privilege, and the quest to make it happen for others.

This, our legacy, demands a constant commitment from those of us who are able to function in a positive and productive manner. We have the right to express an opinion, even to disagree, with no fear of reprisal — but with a sense of well being, respect, and consideration. With a minimum of effort, as easy as breathing, we embrace these rights.

Those without seem unreachable. We see images on television that make us feel helpless. A child in need cannot be pulled out of the tube and held and nurtured. There are words in newspapers about a government in conflict with its own people. It cannot hear the readers' plea to stop aggression and resolve differences. Even if it did, the thought is too simplistic.

My focus, as an illustrator, is on anthropomorphic animals — cats in pajamas, bunnies in top hats, mice in overalls. How can I use them to depict human rights? They seem hardly appropriate for serious thought. Just imagine, however, the acceptance and practice of human rights everywhere! This would evoke feelings of great joy. Joy I can show you with a simple, happy mouse.

Does this seem irreverent? I don't think so. With all of our accomplishments, technology, and the strength of our own good fortune, it is the lack of human rights that I find irreverent.

Iqbal Masih
Jeanette Winter

Iqbal Masih was born into a poor Christian family in the village of Muridke, in Pakistan. When he was only four years old, his parents sold him to a carpet factory for the sum of $16. For the next six years, Iqbal was shackled to a carpet loom. He earned one rupee a day.

At ten, Iqbal was liberated by the Bonded Labor Liberation Front of Pakistan. After he gained his freedom, Iqbal bravely spoke out against child labor. One study has shown that about 1,000,000 children, about 70% of the total work force, work in the carpet industry. It is said that only a child's fingers can give the carpets their beauty.

Iqbal's accounts of the horrors of child labor spread. He traveled far from home to tell his story. Iqbal spoke at an international labor conference in Stockholm. In Boston, he received an award from the Reebok Human Rights Foundation. The United Nations High Commissioner for Human Rights honored Iqbal as a "champion of the fight in Pakistan against contemporary forms of slavery which affects millions of children worldwide."

At home Iqbal received death threats from people in the carpet industry. As he and two cousins rode their bicycles in their village on the Easter Sunday of April 16, 1995, Iqbal was shot and killed. He was twelve years old. The circumstances of his death are unresolved.

CHAUN
Ed Young

MY NEIGHBOR BILLY was caring for his elderly mother when I moved next door to his mother's house. He was perplexed as to why it had been easier for his parents, a blue-collar worker and his wife, to raise five successful children through the years of the Great Depression than it was for those same five grown children to care, in return, for their parents in relatively better times. His perplexity points to our unwillingness to serve the generation before us. It reveals the lack of a principle concerning those in power and those under their care be it in nature or in human relationships.

Inherent rights and privileges are represented in Chinese by the character pronounced "Chuan." "Chuan" is also the name of a standard weight used on a Chinese scale. An object is placed on a tray on one end of a rod marked with measures while the "Chuan" is slid along the other end until the rod achieves a perfect balance. This gives a reading of the object's correct weight.

In human affairs, "balance" is crucial. Power is maintained by balance through flexibility, caring, and sensibility, no matter how small or great the matter to be weighed. When ignorance and greed pervade, those in control become oblivious to the needs of those under them. Such imbalance brings about all manner of violence. In the order of virtues, as quoted in Chapter 38 of *Te Tao Ching*, Laotzu said

> When the way is lost only then do we have virtue;
> When virtue is lost only then do we have humanity;
> When humanity is lost only then do we have righteousness;
> When righteousness is lost only then do we have propriety;
> As for propriety it's but the thin edge of loyalty and sincerity,
> And the beginning of disorder...

Overextension of a one-sided right inevitably violates the rights of others. Independence without a sense of humility becomes self-involvement and inconsideration. Only when our hearts and our minds reside in unison can we address all issues of injustice on earth, in depth and with effectiveness.

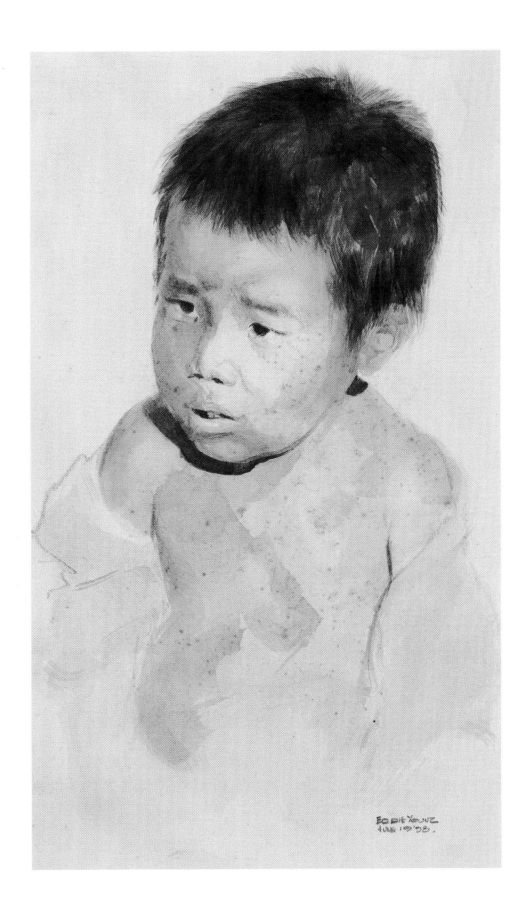

BIOGRAPHIES

Natalie Babbitt

I was born in Ohio in 1932, a time that wasn't quite so innocent as we like to remember. The Depression, the rise of Nazi Germany, and other factors gave the decade an underbelly that was by no means firm. My parents, my sister, and I drew together into a tight protective circle and kept the dangerous outside world at bay as much as we could. We read, we drew pictures, we had music and plenty of laughter, and I decided in the fourth grade to become an illustrator of children's books when I grew up.

I have had a lucky life—good education, happy marriage, fine children, health, a productive career, but I know how changeable fortune can be. The stories I have written all reflect an acceptance of the dark and light sides of life which were so apparent to me when I was a child. In spite of this, however, I have kept my belief in happy endings.

Leonard Baskin

Leonard Baskin, a Caldecott Honor artist, has been a dominant figure in the art world for more than forty years. His recent public sculptural commissions include the Ann Arbor Holocaust Memorial and the FDR Memorial in Washington, DC. A fifty year retrospective of his Gehenna Press fine art books was recently held at the Library of Congress. His printwork and watercolors are in the permanent collections of most of the world's major museums, including the Metropolitan Museum of Art, the Museum of Modern Art, the Smithsonian, and the Vatican Museum. Mr. Baskin's most recent children's books, both collaborations with Richard Michelson, are *Animals That Ought to Be* and *Did You Say Ghosts?* that was selected as one of the New Yorker's fifteen best children's books of the year. He has received numerous awards and honors, among them a Guggenheim Fellowship and the Medal of the American Institute of Graphic Arts. He lives in Leeds, Massachusetts.

Eric Carle

Born in Syracuse, New York, Eric Carle received much of his education in Germany. After graduating from the Akademie der bildenden Künste in Stuttgart, he returned to the United States to work as a designer for the *New York Times*. He later became an art director for a large international advertising agency.

In 1968 Mr. Carle illustrated his first children's book, *Brown Bear Brown Bear What Do You See?*, written by Bill Martin Jr. "When I first began to think about children's books, it reawakened in me struggles of my own childhood in Germany, touching an unfinished area of my own growing up. A child spends five years basically at home — a place of warmth, play and protection. Then school begins, and all of a sudden it is a world of schedule, abstraction, and organized learning. I decided I wanted to create books that make this transition easier." He has been creating children's books ever since.

Mr. Carle has two grown children, and lives with his wife, Barbara, in western Massachusetts.

NORMAND L. CHARTIER

NORMAND CHARTIER is a native Connecticut artist. A watercolorist and illustrator, he has received accolades in both idioms. His paintings, which have won numerous awards, have found their way into both public and private collections throughout the country. He is an elected artist member of the Mystic Art Association. As an illustrator, Mr. Chartier specializes in children's book art. He has illustrated fifty-five books to-date and his work has appeared in *Cricket, Lady Bug, Spider,* and *Sesame Street* magazines. Critical acclaim and awards in this field have been numerous. In 1996 his illustrations for *A Mouse in Solomon's House* were awarded the Gold Medallion in the picture book category from the Evangelical Christian Publishers Association. Mr. Chartier has been selected to contribute to the New York Society of Illustrators' Original Art Exhibition three times. He is listed in *Something About the Author* (Gale Research) and in *The Very Best of Children's Book Illustration* (North Light Books). He is also a member of the Society of Children's Book Writers and Illustrators.

VICTORIA CHESS

VICTORIA CHESS was born in Chicago, Illinois in 1939; her family moved to Washington, Connecticut when she was two. She attended the local kindergarten and grammar school until the age of eight, when with her parents, she moved to Paris. For a part of that time she lived with the Swiss nanny who had taken care of her as a baby and attended a small one room schoolhouse in Switzerland. Then she returned to Connecticut and to the same school, same, friends, same life. Next she was sent to the Mary C. Wheeler School for Girls (from 1954 until 1958), followed by a year at La Châtèlaine in Switzerland, also for girls. Then came two years at the Boston Museum School of Fine Arts followed by a return to Switzerland for a year; and, then, life, jobs, marriage, and one son in New York.

Ms. Chess illustrated her first book in 1965. Following what seems to be her life's pattern, in 1972 they moved to Washington, DC; then to Beirut, Lebanon; and, in 1974, back to Washington, Connecticut. Divorce, life plenty of books to do, same old friends, and a nice second husband filled her life. She is now living quite happily in Connecticut, but has just bought a house in France and is hoping to go there for good. It's really where her heart belongs.

ETIENNE DELESSERT

FOR MORE THAN thirty years, self-taught artist Etienne Delessert has been translating his — and the world's — ideas, passions, fantasies, and nightmares into the visual language of books and magazine illustrations, posters, animated films, and paintings. He delights both children and adults with his creatures and landscapes, in which he juxtaposes the familiar with the fantastic to clarify this world and create new and lasting universes.

Mr. Delessert has illustrated numerous children's books, from his groundbreaking *The Endless Party* and influential collaborations with Eugène Ionesco and Jean Piaget, to his own award-winning *A Long Long Song, Ashes, Ashes,* and *Dance!* His illustrations have appeared in leading magazines and newspapers including the *Atlantic Monthly, Rolling Stone* and the *New York Times.* His animated films include the adventures of the endearing Yok-Yok and creations for "Sesame Street." Throughout his career, Delessert's books, fine art, advertising, and poster illustrations have won acclaim around the world. In 1975, his one-man retrospective hung at the Musée des Arts Décoratifs, in the Louvre.

A recent retrospective has toured the United States. It was originated by the Palazzo delle Esposizioni in Rome, then traveled to Bologna, Lausanne, Paris, Montreal, Birmingham, Philadelphia, Provo at Brigham Young University, and Lawrence at Kansas University before coming in 1994 to the Library of Congress in Washington, DC, and New York.

Born in 1941 in Switzerland, he now lives in Lakeville, Connecticut, with his wife Rita Marshall and their young son Adrien.

Tomie dePaola

Tomie dePaola was born in Meriden, Connecticut on September 15, 1934. He received his BFA from Pratt Institute, his MFA from California College of Arts and Crafts, and a doctoral equivalency from Lone Mountain College.

Mr. dePaola is best known for his works for children. Since 1965, he has written and/or illustrated nearly 200 books. He has received virtually every significant recognition for his books in the children's book world, including the Caldecott Honor Award from the American Library Association. His artwork has been exhibited worldwide, including at the Art Institute of Chicago.

Jane Dyer

As far back as I can remember, I wanted to be a teacher. My mother taught kindergarten so I grew up in a house filled with art projects, music, and books. I laugh when I recall the hours I spent playing school with my cat and dog. I would dress them up and conduct classes in reading and writing. While I had little real success with my earliest students, I went on to become an innovative and successful teacher. Art, music, and literature were incorporated into many of the activities of my kindergarten and second grade classes.

It was my students' parents as well as my family and friends who encouraged me to give up teaching in order to pursue a career in children's book illustration. I found my first publishing job with the Boston Educational Research Company, where I wrote and illustrated teacher's guides for a new reading program that was being developed. A special gift for illustration soon led to trade book work for numerous publishers. My first work was for simple board books, such as *Moo, Moo, Peekaboo,* published by Random House in 1986. From that modest beginning I embarked on a colorful career, during which I have created many books that have become children's classics. Among those are two that received Parent's Choice Honor Book awards for illustration, *Piggins* and *The Three Bears Rhyme Book;* and the highly acclaimed *Time for Bed,* written by Mem Fox. Recently I collaborated with my long-time friend and colleague, Jane Yolen, on *Child of Faerie.*

I live in Northampton, Massachusetts, with my two daughters, Brooke and Cecily, my husband, Tom, our three cats, and Wooly the Wheaten Terrier.

CATHRYN FALWELL

CATHRYN FALWELL, author and illustrator of many picture books, was born in Kansas and spent her early childhood in the midwest before moving to Connecticut. A printmaking major, she received a BA in Art from the University of Connecticut's School of Fine Arts in 1975.

Ms. Falwell was a teacher and a freelance graphic designer in New Hampshire for several years. Returning to Connecticut, she worked as an art director and designer for an award-winning graphic design firm. In 1983 she established her own design business in Hartford, specializing in institutional and corporate print design.

After her second child was born, she decided to pursue the children's book field - something she had wanted to do since the second grade. Her first book, Where's Nicky?, was published in 1991. Other of her books include *Feast for 10, Dragon Tooth,* and *The Letter Jesters.*

Ms. Falwell now lives in Gorham, Maine, with her husband, Peter Mirkin, and their sons, Alexander and Nicholas.

TOM FEELINGS

TOM FEELINGS WAS born and grew up in Brooklyn, and attended the School of Visual Arts. He has traveled throughout the Caribbean, East Africa, and West Africa, where he lived in Ghana. He has also lived in Guyana, South America, where he trained young artists in book illustration for the government.

Mr. Feelings has put his art into service forging and deepening new knowledge concerning African and African American cultures in the Diaspora. The awards for his outstanding illustrations include the Caldecott Honor Book (1972) for *Moja Means One,* the Caldecott Honor Book (1974) for *Jambo Means Hello,* the School of Visual Arts Outstanding Achievement Alumni Award, four Coretta Scott King Awards, the Multicultural Publishers Exchange Award, and an American Book Award nomination (1982). He was also the recipient of a National Endowment for the Arts fellowship in 1982.

In 1995, Feelings won his fourth Coretta Scott King Award for *The Middle Passage,* which explores the story of the cruel and terrifying forced journey of enslaved Africans across the Atlantic Ocean. It is a "wordless book" illustrated in sixty dramatic black-and-white narrative paintings.

"When I am asked what kind of work I do, my answer is that I am a storyteller, in picture form, who tries to reflect and interpret the lives and experiences of the people that gave me life. When I am asked who I am, I say that I am an African who was born in America. This answer connects me specifically with my past and present. I therefore bring to my art a quality that is rooted in the culture of Africa and is expanded by the experience of being black in America. I use the vehicle of 'fine art' and 'illustration' as a viable expression of form, yet strive always to do this from an African perspective, an African world view, and above all to tell the African story. The struggle to create artwork, as well as to live creatively under any conditions and, like my ancestors, survive embodies my particular heritage in America."

Leonard Everett Fisher

Leonard Everett Fisher graduated from the Yale Art School following his World War II military service. In a career spanning more than forty years, he has illustrated some two hundred fifty books for young readers, authoring eighty of these. His published works have appeared in seventeen languages worldwide. In addition, he has designed a number of United States postage stamps. Among the honors he has received are a Pulitzer Prize painting scholarship, the Primio Grafico Fiera Internazionale di Bologna, Medallion of the University of Southern Mississippi, Christopher Medal, National Jewish Book Award, Regina Medal of the Catholic Library Association, Kerlan Award of the University of Minnesota, and the American Library Association's Arbuthnot Lecture citation. His paintings and illustrations can be seen in public collections nationwide, including those of the University of Connecticut.

Antonio Frasconi

Antonio Frasconi was born in Buenos Aires in 1919 to Italian parents. In that same year the family moved to Montevideo, where Frasconi first exhibited his drawings in 1939. He worked as a political cartoonist for two weekly newspapers in Montevideo and exhibited monotypes and woodcuts there in 1944. In 1945 he came to the United States on a scholarship from the Art Students League of New York. He has taught at a number of institutions including the New School for Social Research and the State University of New York at Purchase. Widely respected as a graphic artist, he has exhibited at the Santa Barbara Museum of Art, the Brooklyn Museum, the Cleveland Museum of Art, the Baltimore Museum of Art, the Cooper-Hewitt Museum, the American Institute of Graphic Arts, and the Grolier Society. *The House That Jack Built* was selected as a Caldecott Honor Book in 1959 and as one of the American Institute of Graphic Arts' Children's Books for 1958-1960. Mr. Frasconi's work, including *Twelve Fables of Aesop* (1955) and *The Cantilever Rainbow* (1965), has been consistently selected for inclusion in the American Institute of Graphic Arts prestigious 50 Books of the Year.

Mr. Frasconi represented Uruguay at the 34th Biennale Internazionale d'Arte in Venice, and, in 1969, was named National Academician by the National Academy of Design. He is the subject of Nat Hentoff's monograph, *Frasconi — Against the Grain.*

MARYLIN HAFNER

I WAS BORN in Brooklyn into a large family of artists and musicians. My father, who was a painter, kept me supplied with crayons, pastels, and paper. I knew he hoped I would follow in his footsteps, but I was as strongly influenced by the beautifully printed and illustrated books handed down by older siblings.

The Depression changed our lives. My mother went to work and, as we grew older, my sisters and I knew we too would have to earn a living. I won a scholarship to Pratt Institute, which was known then as a "commercial" art school. Fortunately for me, the faculty were émigrés from Bauhaus Europe and my teachers helped me get jobs while I was a student. A broad range of experience in art-related fields was encouraged.

I designed store displays and textiles, and took advertising assignments. On graduation I became an art director at McCall's Magazine. Marriage and children changed my focus, but I continued working in editorial and advertising illustration. Deadlines were short, so I could fit jobs into my domestic routine.

My husband died while my daughters were still in school. I supported them by teaching art in a school near home. When I had the opportunity to join an art studio that represented book illustrators, I was able to quit teaching.

Illustrating books has occupied me continuously for thirty years. I've worked for the children's magazine CRICKET since its very beginning and I created the characters Molly and Emmet for LADYBUG magazine. I sometimes wonder whether, if I hadn't had to make a living at such an early age, I would have pursued a life as a "fine" artist. One thing is certain: I have had the pleasure of working with talented people in the production of books for children to enjoy. One can't ask much more of life!

MICHAEL HAGUE

MICHAEL HAGUE was born in Los Angeles, his parents having emigrated to California from London just after World War II. Greatly influenced by the comics (especially Prince Valiant) when he was growing up, he attributes much of his interest in romantic fantasy to the Prince's adventures.

Mr. Hague received a BFA with honors from the Los Angeles Art Center College of Design. After graduating, he moved to Kansas City, where he spent two years working for Hallmark Cards. He then moved to Colorado Springs to work at the Current Company, where he designed greeting cards and calendars.

Michael Hague has been influenced by a wide variety of artistic styles, ranging from the work of the Disney Studios to the oriental printmakers Hiroshige and Hokusai. He has been particularly influenced by the turn-of-the-century illustrators Arthur Rackham, W. Heath Robinson, N. C. Wyeth, and Howard Pyle, and is an avid collector of their books.

He says of his work, "I count myself as one of the most fortunate of beings. For as an artist I have not only the pleasure but the duty to daydream. It is part of my work. I have been a contented day dreamer all of my life, often to the exasperation of those around me. I have always wanted to be a book illustrator. Books are what got me interested in art in the first place. I try to infuse my illustrations with the same spirit that the author or the story produced in my imagination. I strive to create something from an empty canvas that becomes a whole 'other world' that people can visit for a while and totally believe in. That challenge of bringing a subject to life and making it believable — that's what is exciting to me as an artist. It doesn't matter whether it is a Greek myth or an American legend, my approach is the same — to try and blend fantasy with realism."

Mr. Hague still lives in the Rocky Mountain area with his wife, Kathleen, three children, three cats, a bird, and two large dogs.

LILLIAN HOBAN

LILLIAN HOBAN was born in Philadelphia, the youngest child in a family that loved to read. From an early age she was read to and encouraged to read on her own. In elementary school she was also encouraged to draw and paint in a program for gifted children.

She became determined to be a dancer after seeing a modern dance performance in junior high school. While continuing to study art, she also began to study dance. Upon graduating from high school she was awarded a scholarship and chose to attend the Philadelphia Museum School of Art. After leaving art school she married and moved to New York where she studied dance at the Hanya Holm School. She then danced professionally and taught dance until the birth of her third child.

Ms. Hoban started her career as a children's book illustrator in her mid-thirties and was encouraged to write her own books by Ursula Nordstrom. She has illustrated over 100 books and written more than 30.

She has four children and lives in Connecticut.

NONNY HOGROGIAN

NONNY HOGROGIAN has been drawing or painting since the age of three and has been an illustrator of children's books for 35 years. She won two Caldecott Medals, one in 1966 for *Always Room for One More* by Sorche Nic Leodhas, and the other in 1972 for her own retelling of an Armenian folktale, *One Fine Day.* She married the poet David Kherdian in 1971 and they have collaborated on many creative projects. They now live in Sebastopol, California.

TRINA SCHART HYMAN

TRINA SCHART HYMAN was born in 1939 and grew up in a rural area north of Philadelphia. She attended the Philadelphia College of Art, the Boston Museum School of Fine Arts, and the Swedish School for Applied Art in Stockholm. Her majors were illustration, printmaking, and advertising design. Her first illustrated book for children was published in Sweden in 1961. Since then she has illustrated 120 children's books, four of which she wrote. She has designed hundreds of greeting cards and other such ephemera, and was the art director for CRICKET for its first seven years. Her work has won many awards including, in 1958, the Caldecott Medal for *Saint George and the Dragon*.

She has one grown daughter and two small grandsons. She lives in Northern new Hampshire in a 175-year-old farmhouse with her partner, one dog, two cats, and four sheep.

WILLIAM JOYCE

WILLIAM JOYCE was born on December 11, 1957 in Shreveport, Louisiana, where he now lives with his wife and two children. He began illustrating children's books after graduating from Southern Methodist University and has been doing so ever since. Among other work, he has written and illustrated *George Shrinks, Dinosaur Bob and His Adventures With the Family Lazardo, A Day With Wilbur Robinson, Bently & Egg, Santa Calls*, and *The Leaf Men and the Brave Good Bugs*.

STEVEN KELLOGG

I HAVE LOVED picture books ever since I was a child. The illustrations of Beatrix Potter and N. C. Wyeth were early favorites, and I always found any kind of animal story irresistible. I was an enthusiastic young artist as well. I formulated pre-school plans to make drawing the center of my lifetime career. I used to dream up stories and illustrate them for my younger sisters Patti and Martha. We called the activity: "Telling Stories on Paper." I would sit between them with a stack of paper in my lap, and a pencil in my hand, rattling off tales and scribbling illustrations to accompany them. I then passed the pictures first to one of the girls and then to the other. As I enormously enjoyed these storytelling sessions, I usually persevered until my sisters were too restless to sit there any longer, or were buried under pieces of paper.

I scribbled my way through elementary, junior, and senior high school, and afterward I attended the Rhode Island School of Design, where I majored in illustration. I was particularly intrigued by the few projects we were given that related to the creation of picture books. I was fortunate enough to win a fellowship that made possible a senior year of work and study in Florence, Italy. It was an exciting and fulfilling period for me. I find that I draw constantly on the experiences and images that I stored during my time there.

Upon my return to the United States I did some graduate work and teaching at American University. At the same time, I began submitting picture book ideas to various publishers. It was an exciting moment when the first acceptances came in, and I realized that I would be able to "tell stories on paper" full time and to a much larger audience. I loved the challenge of putting the first books together, guiding them through the various stages of the publishing process, and then watching them disperse into the lives of their readers. Over twenty years, and eighty books, later, I still find every aspect of my involvement just as absorbing and enjoyable.

During the time that I've been working on the picture books, I've lived in an old farmhouse in the hills of Connecticut, which I've shared with my wife, Helen, and where we've raised the six step children to whom most of my books are dedicated. Also in residence have been numerous dogs and cats, including a beloved harlequin Great Dane named Pinkerton, whose stubborn unadaptability to puppyhood inspired the book *Pinkerton, Behave!* The heroine of the sequel, *A Rose for Pinkerton*, is our senior cat, Secondhand Rose, an independent old grouch who was born a wild thing in the Catskill Mountains. She has devoted her long life to harassing everyone in the world, including Pinkerton.

The ideas for my other books come from many different sources, but most of them have their roots in feelings and images that I retain from my own childhood. I try to blend illustrations and words so that each book is a feast for the eye and ear. I want the time that the reader shares with me and my work to be an enjoyable experience that will encourage a lifetime association with pictures, words, and books.

Hilary Knight

Hilary Knight was born in 1926 in Hempstead, Long Island. The son of Clayton and Katherine Sturgis Knight, both of whom were artists and writers, he began his art career with the publication of drawings in House and Garden and Mademoiselle. He has written and illustrated more than ten books for children and has illustrated more than fifty books written by such well-known children's authors as Betty MacDonald, Judith Viorst, and Charlotte Zolotow. Mr. Knight is perhaps best-known for his illustrations for Kay Thompson's *Eloise*, *Eloise in Paris*, *Eloise at Christmas Time*, and *Eloise in Moscow*. He has also designed posters for a number of Broadway plays, including *Half a Sixpence*, *Irene*, and *Sugar Babies*. His work has been included in the annual exhibition The Original Art: Celebrating the Fine Art of Children's Book Illustration at the Major Eagle Gallery.

E. B. Lewis

Comfortable in his role as the "class clown," young Earl Bradley Lewis's shattering moment of truth came when he was a sixth grader seated in the auditorium of a Philadelphia public school. Near the end of one particularly inspiring assembly program, the guest performer asked randomly selected students to tell what they wanted to be when they grew up. Earl's straight-faced, dead-serious answer, "I want to be a lawyer!" caused a general outburst of incredulous laughter that seemed interminable to him. As a result of this embarrassing, but pivotal, moment in his life, Earl made up his mind that, in spite of his reputation, he would show everyone that he could, indeed, become "somebody" and make outstanding contributions to society.

Earl decided upon a career in art. He loved to draw, displayed unusual artistic talent from an early age, and benefited from the tutelage of talented artists and art teachers in his family. In 1975 he enrolled at Temple University's Tyler School of Art where he majored in graphic design and illustration while also studying art education.

Upon graduation from Tyler, he began teaching, freelancing in graphic design, and painting. An outstanding watercolorist, Mr. Lewis' award winning works have been exhibited and sold out in prestigious galleries nationwide since 1985. His art is also included in many distinguished collections including those of the Pew Charitable Trust and First Pennsylvania Bank.

Not until 1994 did he finally decide to try his hand at illustrating children's books. Based upon the extensive portfolio he submitted, he was assigned to illustrate, as his first book, Jane Kurtz' *A Fire on the Mountain*. Since then, based on his superb, authentic illustrations for that book, he has been commissioned by several major publishers to illustrate at least three books a year. E. B. has won countless accolades and honors for his work as an illustrator of such children's books as *The New King* (1995), *Big Boy* (1995), *Down the Road* (1995), *The Magic Moonberry Jump Ropes* (1996), and *Magid Fasts for Ramadan* (1996).

ANITA LOBEL

ANITA LOBEL was born in Cracow, Poland, just before the beginning of World War II. In the proper Jewish household in which she lived there were several servants. Among them was Anita's beloved nanny. She had taken care of Anita and her younger brother since their birth. It was this strong-willed Catholic country woman who guarded Anita and her brother, passing them off as her own children. They spent five years being carted from town to village until they were discovered hiding in a convent. The two children were taken to a concentration camp. Somehow they survived until the liberation. They were then taken to Sweden. Eventually, Anita's parents were found and the family was reunited in Stockholm. There Anita went to high school and began taking art lessons. When the family emigrated to New York, Anita won a scholarship to Pratt Institute.

There she met and married Arnold Lobel. Anita became a textile designer, working at home while their two children were growing up. One Christmas she gave Susan Hirschman, then Arnold Lobel's editor, three small scarves that she had made from some of the intricate flowery prints in which she specialized. Susan suggested she do a picture book. *Sven's Bridge*, which was published in 1965, made the *New York Times'* best illustrated list that fall, and, redesigned in full color, it was reissued by Greenwillow in 1992.

Ms. Lobel soon discovered that she could combine the exuberance of decoration inherent in her fabric designs with the continuity found in the narrative structure of picture books. She has illustrated many over the years. Some were texts written for Anita by Arnold, including *The Rose in my Garden, On Market Street,* and *A Treeful of Pigs.* Others were adaptations from Scandinavian folk stories, including *The Pancake, Straw Maid,* and *King Rooster, Queen Hen.*

Some of Anita's most challenging and favorite works have been *Princess Furball* and *Toads and Diamonds* by Charlotte Huck, and *This Quiet Lady* by Charlotte Zolotow, as well as her own alphabet books — *Alison's Zinnia, Away from Home,* and *The Dwarf Giant,* which was inspired by Japanese theater.

Anita's interest in theater, music, and foreign languages has served her well in her work as a picture and story maker. She has designed clothes, and stained glass windows, and embroidered tapestries. She has also been an actress and a singer. "It is the 'drama' in a picture book text that interests me the most," says Anita. "I 'stage' the text the way a director might work on a theater piece. Even though I have been involved with picture books for many years, with each new text I tackle, be it written by myself or by someone else, I am always looking for a new 'vision'. In the past few years full color printing techniques have been so improved that I have had a chance to rediscover the way I wanted to paint pictures when I was a young student in art school."

THOMAS LOCKER

THOMAS LOCKER was born, in 1937, in New York and grew up in Washington, DC. He attended the University of Chicago and graduated with a BA in Art History, then earned an MA in Art from American University in Washington, DC. He taught at small colleges in the Midwest before becoming a full time fine artist. His work has been exhibited at one-man shows in New York, London, Chicago, San Francisco, and Atlanta, including two one-man exhibitions at Hammer Galleries in New York. In 1984 he began a new career in the illustration of children's books. Since that time he has illustrated over twenty books. He now lives in a village at the edge of the Hudson River in upstate New York. Mr. Locker has five sons.

BETSY & GIULIO MAESTRO

BETSY AND GIULIO MAESTRO have been creating books together since 1974. They are well known in the publishing field for their non-fiction, which is characterized by their attention to detail and the clarity of both words and pictures. Their consistent, accessible approach has been well received by both reviewers and educators. The Maestros have collaborated on more than seventy books. The American Story series for Lathrop, Lee & Shepard began with their highly acclaimed *The Discovery of the Americas.* This ongoing series continues to help young readers understand and connect events in our nation's history. Their latest book, *The Story of Religion* (Clarion Books), is an introduction to the history of religious belief and the practice of religion throughout today's world.

Betsy Maestro was a kindergarten and first grade teacher for eleven years before beginning her writing career. She has a degree in Early Childhood Education and a Master's degree in counseling. Giulio Maestro graduated from Cooper Union in New York city with a Bachelor's degree in Fine Arts. He worked in advertising for five years before turning his hand to book illustration. Since 1969, he has illustrated more than one hundred books for young readers. He is also author of a number of stories and riddle books.

Many of the Maestros' books have been chosen as Notable Books by the American Library Association, and as Pick of the Lists by the American Bookseller's Association. Giulio Maestro's illustrations have been exhibited by the American Institute of Graphic Arts, the New York Society of Illustrators, and the Art Director's Club of New York.

The Maestros live in Old Lyme, Connecticut with their two children, Daniela and Marco.

MARIANNA MAYER

MARIANNA MAYER was born in New York City. Her educational training focused on art, theology, and music. After receiving a Fine Arts degree, she continued painting studies at the Art Students League. The Pre-Raphaelite narrative artists of the nineteenth century along with the time/relativity obsessed Surrealists of the twentieth century were major influences on her work. Her most important role model was the great champion of human rights, William Morris, who offered her an understanding of how art can shape the world — politically, socially, environmentally, and spiritually.

Very early in her career Ms. Mayer shifted from fine art to book illustration and writing. Her first children's book was published when she was 19 years old. Since then her work within the field of children's book publishing has encompassed art direction, design, editorial work, illustration, production, publishing, and writing. The thematic concerns that she seeks to address in her work deal with myth, folklore, and legend as they relate to transcendence, and most importantly, humankind's struggle with that which is elemental and irrefutable. Her focus is on young people and art. There she concentrates on the idea that art educates, and that wisdom, truth, and compassion can be learned through the application and understanding of art .

She has lived the last 24 years in the northwestern hills of Roxbury in Litchfield County, Connecticut. In the company of dogs and horses, her time is spent writing and illustrating. Her home is a once working 18th century colonial farm with fields, woodland, and pastures that roll gently down to the banks of the rocky river named by Native Americans the Shepaug.

Emily Arnold McCully

I was born July 1, 1939 in Galesburg, Illinois to a former actress and a writer/producer of documentary and public affairs radio programs. I grew up outside New York City.

At three I learned to read and made efforts at representational drawing, which my mother encouraged, seeing commercial art as a potential career. My pictures were usually tied to texts — favorite stories or ones I wrote myself. I was already an illustrator.

At college, I drifted away from drawing but majored in art history, wrote fiction and theater pieces, and acted. When I had to find a job, my literary ambitions outstripped my qualifications. For a while I cut mats in an ad agency. Out of frustration I assembled a portfolio of drawings, took it around to art directors, and, eventually, began to get modest commissions for book covers and advertisements. My poster for a radio station was spotted by a children's editor at Harper & Row who gave me a manuscript to illustrate. I became an illustrator of children's books while writing an O'Henry Prize story and two novels for adults. Finally, I created a children's book of my own. That book, *The Wordless Picnic*, won a Christopher Award. Since then I've written and illustrated picture books exclusively.

I have focused on stories about able, daring girls who persevere. As a child I wished I had been born male, because so much more of life seemed available to boys. While that has changed a great deal, adventure stories about girls still seem to be in short supply. I have also been writing books about real historical events of importance — Elizabeth Cady Stanton's suffrage campaign, a turnout at the Lowell Mills, Granuaile's battle with the English — that show women affecting the course of history and that allow me to use narrative to excite the imagination.

Michael McCurdy

Michael McCurdy was born in New York City in 1942. He was graduated from the Boston School of the Museum of Fine Arts and Tufts University. Along with his work as an illustrator, he has written several books. These include *The Devils Who Learned to be Good, Hannah's Farm, The Old Man and the Fiddle*, and *Trapped by the Ice: Shackleton's Amazing Journey*. He edited and illustrated Frederick Douglass' first autobiography, renamed *Escape from Slavery: The Boyhood of Frederick Douglass in His Own Words*. His wood engravings and drawings are found in trade books and limited editions for both adults and children. Among the fine press editions that Mr. McCurdy has illustrated are *The Winged Life* (H. D. Thoreau), *My First Summer in the Sierra* (John Muir), and *American Buffalo* (David Mamet). McCurdy is listed in *Who's Who in America* and *Who's Who in American Art.*

LAUREN MILLS

LAUREN MILLS was born in 1957, the fourth of five children. She grew up in Connecticut, Oregon, and Minnesota. Her father was a documentary film maker and her mother was a designer. Both later became counselors of alcoholics. This influenced Lauren's decision to study child and family psychology at Gustavus Adolphus College in Minnesota. At the same time she pursued her interest in art and literature. She received a BA in Art from the University of California at Santa Barbara. After working as a fashion illustrator, she returned to school and received a Master's Degree in Book Illustration from San Jose State University where she met her husband, author/illustrator Dennis Nolan. After moving back east, Lauren taught at the Paier College of Art in Connecticut and began illustrating children's classics, including *At the Back of the North Wind* and *Anne of Green Gables*. *The Rag Coat* was her first original story. It received the Charlotte Award, has been told over the radio, and has been performed as a ballet and a play. Her work has been exhibited in museums and galleries throughout the country, including the National Museum of Women in the Arts. Lauren and her husband and young daughter live in a converted barn in the Berkshires of Massachusetts.

WENDELL MINOR

WENDELL MINOR is well known in the publishing industry for the paintings he has done for children's books and for the jackets of many best selling novels, including David McCullough's *Truman* and Pat Conroy's *Beach Music*. Mr. Minor has received over 200 awards from every major graphics competition, including silver medals from the Society of Illustrators and the New York Art Directors Club. He has been featured in articles in PRINT MAGAZINE, AMERICAN ARTIST, and IDEA MAGAZINE of Japan.

In 1988 Mr. Minor was chosen as one of a six-member team commissioned by NASA to document the shuttle Discovery's return to flight. In 1989 he created North Dakota's Centennial stamp for the US Postal Service. He also created two postal card stamps for the Scenic America series: "Niagara Falls" in 1991, and "Red Barn" in 1995.

As President of the Society of Illustrators from 1989 to 1991, Mr. Minor organized an international exhibition **Art for Survival: The Illustrator and the Environment** and oversaw the subsequent publication of the book of the same name. In 1995 Harcourt Brace and Company published *Wendell Minor: Art For the Written Word*, a retrospective of twenty five years of Mr. Minor's book cover art. That book includes commentary from over 60 authors and a selection of over one hundred paintings of his paintings for books by Pat Conroy, Louise Erdich, Fannie Flagg, John Hersey, Tracy Kidder, James Michener, Anton Myrer, Elizabeth Marshall Thomas, and Judith Rossner, among others. Mr. Minor has recently contributed art and commentary to *On the Wings of Peace: Writers and Illustrators Speak Out for Peace, in Memory of Hiroshima and Nagasaki*.

Mr. Minor has had numerous solo exhibitions, and his work can be found in the permanent collections of the Muskegon Museum of Art, the Mazza Collection at the University of Findlay, the Illinois State Museum, the Library of Congress, and the Museum of American

Illustration; as well as in the art collections of NASA, the U. S. Coast Guard, and the U. S. Air Force.

BARRY MOSER

BARRY MOSER was born in Chattanooga, Tennessee in 1940. He was educated early on at a military academy there, the Baylor School, then at Auburn University and the University of Tennessee at Chattanooga. He later did graduate work at the University of Massachusetts at Amherst. He studied with George Cress, Leonard Baskin, Fred Becker, and Jack Coughlin. His work is represented in numerous collections, museums, and libraries in the United States and abroad, including the National Gallery of Art, the Metropolitan Museum, the British Museum, the Library of Congress, the Newark Public Library, the National Library of Australia, the London College of Printing, Harvard University, Yale University, Dartmouth College, Cambridge University, and Princeton University to name a few. Mr. Moser has exhibited internationally in both one-man and group exhibits. He is a member of the Society of Printers, Boston, and was elected an Associate of the National Academy of Design in 1982 and a full Academician in 1994. He is on the faculty of the Illustration Department at the Rhode Island School of Design and was the 1995 Whitney J. Oates Fellow in Humanities at Princeton University. The books Moser has illustrated and/or designed over 200 titles including the Arion Press *Moby-Dick* and the University of California Press edition of Dante's *The Divine Comedy*. Moser's edition of Lewis Carroll's *Alice's Adventures in Wonderland*, won the National Book Award for design and illustration in 1983.

DENNIS NOLAN

DENNIS NOLAN was born in San Francisco in 1945. His father was an operatic tenor and his early childhood memories of backstage, makeup, costumes, and performances helped to create a lifelong interest in dramatic and colorful storytelling. After attending Bay Area schools, he earned a BA degree in Art History and an MA degree in painting from San Jose State University. A variety of jobs followed, including painting for galleries, illustrating biology text books, and animating films. He also taught illustration at San Jose State University and the University of Hartford in Connecticut.

Mr. Nolan's first book was published in 1976. Ever since he has been captivated by the telling of stories in words and pictures. Several of the books that he has written and illustrated have been singled out for recognition. Among them are *The Castle Builder*, winner of the Prix de Zephir in France; and *Dinosaur Dream*, a season's best choice in both Newsweek and the New Yorker, and an SCBWI Golden Kite Honor Book. He has illustrated T. H. White's classic *The Sword in the Stone* along with numerous other books including titles by Jane Yolen, Dianne Stanley, and William Hooks. He has also collaborated with his wife, author and illustrator Lauren Mills, on the illustrations for her story *Fairy Wings*, and has illustrated Bruce Coville's retelling of William Shakespeare's *A Midsummer Night's Dream*.

Robert Andrew Parker

Robert Andrew Parker was born in 1927 in Norfolk, Virginia. He studied at the School of the Art Institute of Chicago, Skowhegan School of Painting and Sculpture in Maine, and Atelier 17 in New York City. He has taught at Skowhegan, the School of Visual Arts in New York City and Gerit Rietveld Academie in Amsterdam, The Netherlands.

Mr. Parker has been a Guggenheim Fellow and has received a Rosenthal Foundation Grant, as well as the Ranger Purchase Prize from the National Academy of Design. His work is held by the Brooklyn Museum, Dublin Museum in Ireland, Los Angeles County Museum, Metropolitan Museum of Art, Museum of Modern Art, and other institutions.

He currently lives and works in West Cornwall, CT. His *Franz Kafka: Dreams, Diaries and Fragments* (Four Winds Fine Art, 1994) offers a larger selection of his images of Kafka's work.

Gloria Jean Pinkney

Gloria Jean Pinkney was born in Lumberton, North Carolina, the site of her first book for children, *Back Home*. Her second book *The Sunday Outing*, which is a prequel to *Back Home*, takes place in Philadelphia, Pennsylvania, where she was raised.

Over the years, Ms. Pinkney has collaborated with her husband, illustrator Jerry Pinkney in making books for children. Her recognition includes a Parent's Choice Award (1992), an American Library Association Notable Children's Book citation, and a United Nations Society of Writers' award.

In addition to writing and working with her spouse, Gloria Jean has been an arts and crafts instructor. She is also a silversmith and designer of ladies' hats. Her millinery designs have been exhibited in several Westchester County galleries. For the past five years, she has toured the country speaking to children and adults about the making of picture books.

Jerry Pinkney

Jerry Pinkney has illustrated more than 75 books for children and twenty for adults. He is the recipient of numerous awards, including three Gold Medals from the New York Society of Illustrators, three Caldecott Honor Books, three Coretta Scott King Awards, and the *New York Times'* Best Illustrated Book for 1989 and 1994. He has received the 1992 Alumni Award from the University of the Arts in Philadelphia. He has also been honored for his work with a Citation for Children's Literature from Drexel University, and with the David McCord Children's Literature Citation from Framingham State College. Mr. Pinkney has had one man shows in museums and galleries across the United States and has participated in group shows in Europe, Japan, and Russia.

Mark Podwal

Mark Podwal is the author and illustrator of numerous books including, *Golem: A Giant Made of Mud*, and *The Book of Tens*—both for young readers. He has collaborated with Elie Wiesel on various projects, including *A Passover Haggadah* and the video *A Passover Seder*, which was broadcast on public television.

Mr. Podwal's drawings have appeared in the *New York Times* for more than twenty years. His drawings have been exhibited in the Louvre in Paris, the Jewish Museum in New York City, and other museums. In 1993 he was named Chevalier de l'Ordre des Arts et des Lettres de la République Française.

Anita Riggio

Anita Riggio has illustrated nearly twenty books for children including *The Whispering Cloth* by Pegi Deitz Shea. She is the author and illustrator of several picture books, among them, *A Moon in My Teacup* and *Beware the Brindlebeast*, which was awarded a 1995 Picture Book honor by Parent's Choice.

Before she established her career as a writer and illustrator, Ms. Riggio taught Language and Art at the American School for the Deaf in West Hartford, Connecticut. She is currently a participant in the nationally recognized Partners Program (Partners in Arts and Education Revitalizing Schools) sponsored by the Bushnell.

Ruth Sanderson

In 1974 Ruth Sanderson graduated from the Paier College of Art in Hamden, Connecticut. Since then she has illustrated books for children of all ages. Her work is included in textbooks, Golden Books, young adult books, and classics such as *Heidi* and *The Secret Garden*. Since 1989 she has been illustrating fairy tales, among them *The Sleeping Beauty*, as retold by Jane Yolen; *The Twelve Dancing Princesses*, as retold by Sanderson herself; *The Enchanted Wood*, her first original fairy tale; and *Papa Gatto*, an Italian fairy tale. Her work has also appeared on collector's plates, greeting cards, and in editorial and magazine illustrations.

Ms. Sanderson is a member of the Society of Illustrators, the Society of Children's Book Writers, and the Western Massachusetts Illustrator's Guild. She has been a guest speaker at many conferences and schools. *The Enchanted Wood* received the Irma S. Black Award for outstanding picture book of 1991, and the 1995 Young Hoosier Picture Book Award.

Her paintings have been shown in exhibitions around the country, including at the Society of Illustrators, the Delaware Museum of Art, The William King Regional Art Center, The University of Arizona Museum of Art, The Words and Pictures Museum, and The Art Museum of Western Virginia. Six of her paintings were included in The Art of Enchantment exhibit (1995-1996) at the Norman Rockwell Museum. Her other recent picture books are *Beauty and the Beast, Swan Lake, The Tempest*, and *The Nativity*.

URI SHULEVITZ

URI SHULEVITZ was born in Warsaw, Poland, on February 27, 1935. He began drawing at the age of three, and unlike many children, never stopped. The Warsaw blitz occurred when Mr. Shulevitz was four years old. He vividly remembers public services halting, streets caving in, buildings burning, and a bomb falling into the stairwell of his apartment building one day when he was home.

In 1939 the Shulevitz family fled Warsaw. For eight years they were wanderers before arriving in Paris in 1947. There Uri developed an enthusiasm for French comic books. Soon he and a friend began making their own comics, for which Uri drew the pictures. At thirteen he won first prize in an all-elementary-school drawing competition in the 20th district of Paris.

Mr. Shulevitz moved to Israel with his parents and a baby brother in 1949. For two years, he worked during the day at a variety of jobs. From 1952 to 1956 he studied at the Teacher's Institute in Tel Aviv, where he took courses in literature, anatomy, and biology. Uri also studied privately under the painter Ezekiel Shtreichman and at the Art Institute of Tel Aviv. At fifteen, he was the youngest exhibitor in a group drawing show at the Tel Aviv Museum.

During the Sinai War, in 1956, Mr. Shulevitz went into basic training with the Israeli Army and joined the Ein Geddy kibbutz by the Dead Sea. After completing his army service was over, he began a freelance career. At the age of twenty-four he came to New York City.

For the next two years, he studied painting at the Brooklyn Museum Art School and did illustrations for a publisher of Hebrew books for children. One day when talking on the telephone, he noticed that his doodles had a fresh and spontaneous look. They bore no resemblance to the work he was doing for the publisher. This discovery marked the beginning of his new approach to illustration. *The Moon in My Room*, his first book, was published in 1963. Subsequent books include his Caldecott Award winning *The Fool of the World and the Flying Ship Retold*, published in 1969; his more recent books include *Dawn, The Treasure, The Strange and Exciting Adventures of Jeremiah Hush*, and *Toddlecreek Post Office*.

Mr. Shulevitz now lives in Greenwich Village in New York City. He teaches the writing and illustration of children's books.

MARC SIMONT

MARC SIMONT's early years were spent in France, Spain and the United States. At the age of twenty, he settled in the United States. His father was an illustrator and his first teacher. He attended a mix of traditional and unconventional art schools in Paris and New York. His first jobs were assisting mural painters. In 1939 Mr. Simont got his first book illustration job. Since then he has illustrated more than ninety books. His professional work also includes portraits and magazine illustrations. For cathartic reasons he does political cartoons.

Esphyr Slobodkina

Esphyr Slobodkina is a talented painter, sculptor, designer, writer and illustrator of children's books, teacher, and amateur architect. A vivacious and amusing lecturer, she has also appeared on numerous radio and television programs. One of her internationally known stories, *Caps for Sale*, has become recognized as a classic. It has sold millions of copies, been made into a filmstrip, cassette, record, and musical play; it is included in many anthologies.

A founding member of the American Abstract Artists, and of the Federation of Modern Painters and Sculptors, Ms. Slobodkina has had a number of exhibitions of her work. Her paintings are in the permanent collections of the Corcoran Gallery, the Whitney Museum of American Art, the Philadelphia Art Museum, the Metropolitan Museum of New York City, the National Museum of American Art, the New York University, and many other museums.

Miss Slobodkina was born, and spent a very happy childhood, in a pleasant part of Siberia at the foot of the Ural Mountains. Before immigrating to the United States, she lived and studied art in Manchuria. She and her sister now live in Great Neck, Long Island.

Jos. A. Smith

Jos. A. Smith was born in 1936 in Bellefonte, Pennsylvania, and received a BFA degree from the Pratt Institute in Brooklyn in 1958, where he was awarded the Dean's Medal. He is currently a Professor of Fine Art, in the Department of Fine Art, at Pratt Institute, where he has taught since 1962. He has had thirteen solo exhibitions of his drawings, paintings, and sculpture, and has participated in seventy-eight group exhibitions nationwide. Mr. Smith has served as a political cartoonist for Time and Newsweek and as courtroom artist for the Watergate trials for Newsweek. He has illustrated limited edition books for the Franklin Library, magazine illustrations for Harper's New Times, book jackets, and children's books for Greenwillow, Morrow Jr., McElderry Books, Random House, MacDonald, Grosset & Dunlap, and Scholastic. He is also the author of *The Pen & Ink Book* (1992).

Cyndy Szekeres

Cyndy Szekeres has been a children's book illustrator for 36 years. Her work focuses on books for lapsitters and pre-schoolers. She has illustrated over 100 books including a dozen or more of her own stories. The universal appeal of her work is evident from its having been translated and published in many languages.

Ms. Szekeres and her husband, Gennaro Prozzo, a fine artist and sculptor, share a home and studios in southern Vermont.

Jeanette Winter

I can't remember a time when I didn't love to draw. I still remember the feel of the rough oatmeal paper that I drew on with my deluxe 64-color box of Crayolas while in elementary school in Chicago. At home, if paper wasn't available I drew on the cardboard from laundered shirts, and even on endpapers in books. I loved the smell and look of the crayons with their striped wrappers.

There weren't many books in my house when I was growing up, but I do remember the books of the d'Aulaires, Marguerite de Angeli, Elizabeth Orton Jones, and Robert Lawson from the library. My friends and I also read and traded stacks of comic books. I treasured my collection of Saturday Evening Post covers by Norman Rockwell, whose pictures were magical to me.

During high school, all my free time on Saturdays and during the summer was spent in art classes at the Art Institute of Chicago. Because of a special teacher there, Mr. Jacobson, those years were important in helping me become an artist.

I went to college in Iowa where I enjoyed small town life after growing up in a large city. I married, lived in New York City briefly, then moved to Texas, where our two sons were born and raised. Living in rural Maine was a new experience that had begun to make its way into my books, as have all the years in Texas, and my childhood in Chicago. I now live in Pipe Creek, Texas.

I always knew I wanted to make pictures that told a story. Except for a brief time when, at age ten, I was sure that what I really wanted to be was a ballet dancer. The most important things in my childhood books were the pictures. I loved the information and they details they offered me. The rectangle of the picture was like a window into another world. Now I try to make the kind of pictures I would have liked as a child.

Doing research is one of the best parts of making a book. My drawing table is usually surrounded by books on the subject I'm working on. Photographs are also a research resource. I always carry a camera with me to record specific things for a book, or simply to have a record of things I see that I want to remember. I often find myself going back to pictures I took years ago as a reference for a book in progress.

I listen to music while I work; if possible, to music that fits the theme of the book - Mexican mariachi and accordion music for *Diego*, African American spirituals and work songs for *Follow the Drinking Gourd*, Swedish fiddle music for Klara's *New World*, Christmas music (in the spring!) for *The Christmas Tree Ship*, and cowboy songs for *Cowboy Artist*.

Ed Young

1990 Caldecott Medal winner Ed Young has illustrated over 60 books for children, five of which he has also written. The inspiration for his work can be found in the philosophy of Chinese painting, which teaches the art of enriching the beauty of language through vibrant, yet simple, images. "A Chinese painting is often accompanied by words," he explains. "They are complementary. There are things that words do that pictures never can, and likewise, there are images that words can never describe."

Content and the telling of the tale itself provide Mr. Young with the initial inspiration for his art and with the motivation for page design and sequence. Essential to his work is accuracy in research whether it be illustrating fantasy, folk tale, or fact. He believes that credibility must be established in order to create new and exciting images. Through such images, he hopes to capture his readers' imagination and ultimately, to stimulate some sort of awareness in them.

For Mr. Young, challenge and growth are central in his role as illustrator. It is this quest for growth that caused him to move away from commercial art in the 1960s. He sought a more expansive and more expressive venue. He found what he was looking for in children's books. "I feel that the story has to be exciting and a moving experience for a child," he explains. "Before I become involved in a project, I must be moved. I try to create something exciting. It is my goal to stimulate growth in the reader through his or her active participation."

Ed Young, born in Tientsin, China, grew up in Shanghai and later moved to Hong Kong. He came to the United States as a young man on a student visa. A graduate of the Los Angeles Art Center, he has since taught at Pratt Institute, Yale University, Naropa Institute, and the University of California at Santa Cruz. He currently lives in Hastings-on-Hudson, New York, with his wife and daughter.

THE IMAGES IN TIKVAH WERE EXECUTED BY THE INDIVIDUAL ARTISTS FOR THIS PROJECT

USING VARIOUS MEDIA AND SUNDRY PAPERS AND OTHER SUPPORTS.

THE TYPE USED FOR THE TEXT IS ADOBE GARAMOND, DESIGNED BY ROBERT SLIMBACH AND

PUBLISHED BY ADOBE SYSTEMS INCORPORATED IN 1989. IT IS BASED ON EXTENSIVE RESEARCH

OF ORIGINAL SIXTEENTH-CENTURY GARAMOND SPECIMENS FOUND AT THE PLANTIN-MORETUS

MUSEUM IN ANTWERP. IT IS THE MOST ACCURATE REVIVAL TO DATE.

SPECIAL THANKS ARE OWED TO BARRY AND CARA MOSER FOR CONTRIBUTING THEIR SERVICES

IN THE DESIGN AND PRODUCTION OF TIKVAH.